CADOGAN
guides

Hugh & Paul Cantlie

5 m████████e
otorway

Cadogan Books plc
London House, Parkgate Road,
London SW11 4NQ, UK

Distributed in North America by
The Globe Pequot Press
6 Business Park Road, PO Box 833, Old Saybrook,
Connecticut 06475–0833

Copyright © Hugh and Paul Cantlie 1995
Illustrations © Hugh Cantlie 1995

Book and cover design by Animage
Cover illustrations by Horatio Monteverde
Maps © Cadogan Guides, adapted from original drawings
© Paul Cantlie

Series Editors: Rachel Fielding and Vicki Ingle

Editing: Linda McQueen
Additional research: Toby Bourne
DTP: Kicca Tommasi
Production: Rupert Wheeler Book Production Services

**A catalogue record for this book is available from
the British Library**
ISBN 1–86–0110–31–2

Printed and bound in the UK
by Redwood Books Ltd

Please Note

The authors and publishers have made every effort to ensure the
accuracy of the information in the book at the time of going to
press. However, they cannot accept any responsibility for any loss,
injury or inconvenience resulting from the use of information
contained in this guide.

About the Authors

Hugh Cantlie spent several years, between soldiering and surveying, driving the length and breadth of the land as a commercial traveller in the wine trade. Although in their early years, motorway service stations had already established their pattern and he spent many hours fruitlessly searching for alternatives. He vowed that some day he would try to make life on the motorway more bearable and varied for a new generation of travellers.

Paul Cantlie has been designing something or other ever since an apprenticeship in aero-engines. As a family man he frequently drove from Hampshire to the West Highlands of Scotland and back with a car-load of fractious children eager to scatter in all directions at any service station; even five minutes' relaxation resulted in a 20-minute search to locate and gather them all together again. What he knew he needed was a wayside inn just off a convenient junction.

Acknowledgements

We are very grateful to the various branches of the Highways Agency and the Roads Department of the Scottish Office for their patient assistance throughout this project.

Please help us keep this guide up to date

Try as one may, things get overlooked. If users of this guide have comments to make about included listings or places missing which they feel ought to be included or about errors in our map-making, it will help us refine and improve this guide's future editions if they will notify us, using the reply forms at the back of this book, and earn our gratitude.

Introduction

Champany Inn, Linlithgow

On British motorways it is unusual to drive for more than twenty minutes without passing a service station. They are well-spaced and offer refreshment, fuel, full toilet facilities, telephones, amusement arcades and shops to satisfy the requirements of every motorway user. Despite being franchised to a number of different organisations they are of uniform specification and therefore become uniformly boring, unless you actually like that sort of thing.

This book is dedicated to those who do not.

Introduction

The Purpose of the Guide

Nearly every motorway junction seems to offer the possibility of getting away from the pressure of intensive driving for a short while for a meal or snack in calmer surroundings; it is only the uncertainty of whether such a haven exists or how long it will take to resume the journey that makes us reluctant to risk leaving the motorway.

This guide seeks to remove that uncertainty. It involved us in an exhaustive search of every motorway junction in mainland Great Britain, particularly outside the urban areas. To preserve independence of opinion we travelled anonymously.

The first consideration at each junction was that it should take no more than five minutes from the time of leaving the motorway to be parked at a given listing, so that the time required for a break would not be significantly shorter at a motorway service station.

The second requirement for a mention in this book was the availability of good food, either at lunchtimes, in the evenings or both. Inevitably, a high proportion of the places recommended are pubs, which have been fulfilling the needs of travellers since mediæval times, and long before the first restaurant was even conceived. Various well-known chains of roadhouses have been omitted because we do not feel that their atmosphere is essentially different from what we sought to avoid.

Where appropriate, information about the existence of filling stations, either near to the pubs themselves or on the route from the motorway, has also been included, for the benefit of those who like to refuel their cars as well as themselves. You pay top dollar for fuel on the motorway itself, and wayside filling stations seldom charge as much, so there is generally a significant saving to be made.

The listed entries offer a range of services. All premises have their own car parks unless mention is made. While we have tried to give complete information, pubs do change hands and readers travelling to a deadline may be well advised to ring ahead, using the telephone numbers provided.

The general appearance and atmosphere of places were also taken into account, so a degree of subjective opinion is inevitable. We had to ask ourselves whether we would have wished to be tempted off the motorway to stop at a place like this. If you disagree or have any suggestions of your own, do feel free to write to us; some blank listing sheets are included at the end of this book.

Using the Guide

Road Numbers and their Sequence

Perhaps, when the first motorways were being planned and built, a logical method of numbering them was intended. Evidence of this is to be found on the M1, which begets a tributary in the M18 which in turn begets the M180. In the best British traditions, logic soon gave way to pragmatism, so, while the M25 is a nice rounded number, why was it not designated the M15, since its contact with the M1 is just as solid as it is with the M2? Will the M27, starting as it does deep in the New Forest, ever make contact with the M2 or M26?

Introduction

These exceptions may prove the rule, however, and in a great majority of cases there is a sequence of numbering which has prompted us to group all motorways starting with the figure 1 after the M1, all those starting with 2 after the M2 and so on. This means that there is at least some geographical connection between adjoining motorways through-out the book. Motorway numbers are printed on the top outside corner of each page to enable the reader to riffle through the book until the required road number is reached.

If particular motorway numbers are missing it means only that there was nothing found on that motor-way to justify a stop or, more commonly, that the road is a by-pass or infra-urban motorway link such as the M77.

Two English trunk roads, the A1 and A3, have been upgraded along part of their lengths to motorway standards and are designated A1(M) and A3(M); because they might have been confused with the M1 and M3, which both follow quite different routes, they have been placed at the end of the book. The Scottish A74(M), however, will be redesignated as the M74 which already starts at Glasgow, so it is treated as an integral and sequential part of the M74.

Junction Numbers

We have endeavoured to show junction numbers and directions just as they are posted on the final approach board to each junction, which is generally ½-mile before the turn-off. Occasionally the place names differ depending upon the direction in which the junction is approached, which may account for any discrepancies in this respect.

Introduction

Not every junction of every motorway is shown. We have only listed junctions where we found pubs or restaurants which merited a stop.

Restricted Access Junctions

A number of junctions are listed as having 'restricted access'. This means simply that if you can get off at that junction you may not be able to get back on and vice versa. Where we judged a location to be worth a slight detour, we have included it with a cautionary note or indication of how to pick up the motorway again.

Maps

To make this guide as clear and easy to use as possible, a simple map of almost every junction has been drawn, showing no more than will help the user to find the way to a listed stopping place. Motorways are conventionally printed blue. Boxed blue capital letters represent the locations of places listed in the text. The scale of the diagrams varies but nothing is more than 'five minutes off the motorway'. Filling stations have not been shown, since they will be as readily visible to the user as they were to us. The orientation of all maps is correct, north being at the top of each page.

Children and Dogs

At the moment, by law, no one under the age of 14 is allowed in any room in a pub where alcohol is served. This law is widely ignored and is in the process of being changed. Many pubs have family rooms and gardens which permit children, and landlords tend to make their own rules about what

Introduction

they will allow. Our listings state where children are completely forbidden.

We also listed whether dogs are welcomed, but you should note that, even where they are strictly excluded, an exception will be made for guide dogs.

Food and Prices

The listings in this book give a general indication of the price range you might expect to encounter. The range is based on the average cost of a one-course full meal, such as an 8oz steak with vegetables and potatoes, or salmon with a large salad, and is listed as follows:

££££	over £15
£££	£8–£15
££	£5–£7.99
£	under £5

In almost all pubs, however, is is quite possible to find a range of snacks and sandwiches costing between £1.75 and £3.50. Most pubs nowadays cater for the growing number of vegetarians, and some form of vegetarian dish has been available at every place visited.

London ◀   ▶Leeds   M1

Junctions 7 to 47

The first British motorway to be built, the M1 still compares favourably with those that followed in terms of retaining the driver's interest. The unusually high proportion of concrete surfacing is less pleasant to drive on than asphalt but may account for a lower-than-normal amount of roadworks.

Junction 7 is the motorway merger with the M10.

Junction 42 is the motorway intersection with the M62.

Junctions 43–46 lie within the urban and industrial boundaries of Leeds.

---

9   Whipsnade A5

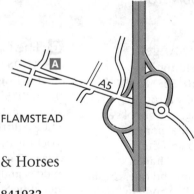

FLAMSTEAD

A Waggon & Horses
Flamstead
℀ (01582) 841932

A picturesque cream-coloured old wayside pub on the busy A5. Coffee and tea, bar food except Sunday and Monday evenings, family room, playground and outside seating. Dogs allowed.

Open for food daily from midday to 10pm (4.30pm Sunday and Monday)
Price: ££
▶ *filling station nearby*

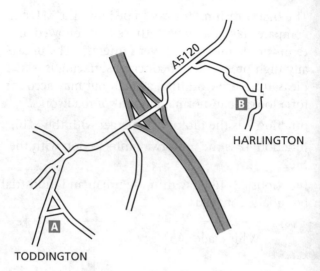

HARLINGTON

TODDINGTON

A The Angel
Toddington
✆ (01525) 873879
Reputedly a 16th-century building, it overlooks an ornamental pond and incorporates the 'Sorrentino' Italian restaurant and café. Cream teas, Italian and English bar meals all week including Sunday evenings. Cheerful appearance.

Open daily from midday to 10pm
Price: ££
▶ *there are a number of other pubs in this attractive village and two filling stations*

B The Carpenter's Arms
Harlington
✆ (01525) 872384
A fine-looking black and white half-timbered coaching inn in a quiet village. Bar meals at midday and evenings including Sunday evenings and an upstairs restaurant. No outside seating and no dogs.

Last orders for weekday meals at 2.15pm and 9.30; 2pm and 9pm on Sundays
Price: ££

13 Milton Keynes (S), Bedford A421, Ampthill A507

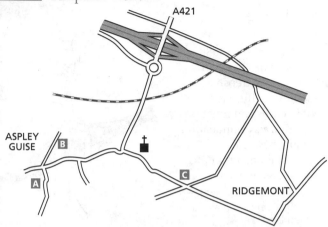

A Moore Place Hotel & The Greenhouse Restaurant
Aspley Guise
✆ **(01908) 282000**

An elegant Georgian mansion in this very attractive village, offering full hotel and restaurant facilities. Children and dogs permitted.

Last orders for meals at 2pm and 9.45pm
Price: ££
▶ *filling station on the road from the junction*

B The Anchor
Aspley Guise
✆ **(01908) 582177**

A pretty white village house converted to a pub serving bar meals except Sunday evenings. Well tended garden.

Last orders 2pm and 9pm; closed for food Sun eves
▶ *specialities: Mexican evening meals*
Price: ££
▶ *filling station on approach to Aspley Guise*

C The White Horse
Woburn
✆ **(01525) 280565**

A white-painted country pub on a road junction facing the wall of the Woburn Estate. Bar meals and snacks with a dining area. Children's playground. No dogs.

Last orders for meals at 2.30pm and 9.30pm
Price: ££–£££
▶ *filling station nearby*

A The Coach Hotel
Moulsoe
℡ (01908) 613688

A handsome Georgian house with extensive additions behind for conferences and functions as well as accommodation. Bar lunches, and a restaurant open for lunch and dinner. No dogs.

Last orders for meals at 2pm and 10pm (9.30pm Sundays)

Price: £££

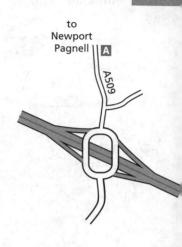

15 Northampton (S and E) A508

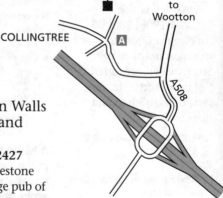

A The Wooden Walls of Old England
Collingtree
℡ (01604) 762427

An attractive rubblestone and thatched village pub of 18th-century appearance. Lounge and saloon bars serving bar menus and snacks including Sunday eves. Closed Christmas Day. Playground and beer garden. No dogs indoors.

Last orders for meals at 2pm and 9.30pm (9pm Sundays)

Price: ££

▶ *filling station on the road from the junction*

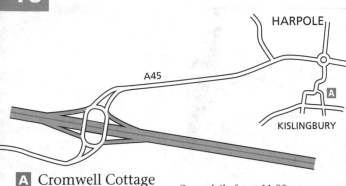

M1

16 Daventry A45

A Cromwell Cottage
Kislingbury
© (01604) 830288

A fine old low-beamed 17th-century house on the banks of the River Nene, with its own sheltered garden and driveway. Upmarket dining area serving lunches and dinners including Sunday evening. Outside seating and a family room. A thoroughly picturesque and comfortable hostelry, worth visiting.

Open daily from 11.00am (midday Sundays) until 9.45pm; food served all day
Price: ££
▶ *filling station on the road from the junction*

18 Daventry A428

A Half Way House
Nr Kilsby
© (01788) 822888

A 1930s public house on a busy intersection with the A5. Breakfasts, coffee and bar snacks. Large beer garden, playground and car park. Dogs allowed.

Open, amazingly, from 7am to 11pm daily; food served all day
Price: £
▶ *filling station opposite*

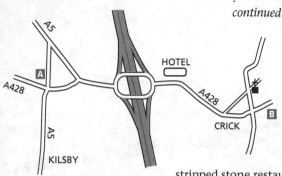

B The Red Lion
Crick
✆ (01788) 822265

A pleasant stone and thatched village inn on a site dating from 1066. Bar with log fires in winter; meals served in a comfortable, low-beamed stripped stone restaurant. Children's playground and outside grassed eating area. Children admitted for lunch, and well-behaved dogs allowed.

Last orders for meals at 1.45pm and 9pm; closed Mondays

Price: ££

▶ *filling station on the road from the junction*

---

29 Chesterfield A617

A The Elm Tree
Heath
✆ (01246) 850490

A good stone-built house in an attractive village with a fine view to the north. Hot and cold bar food at lunchtime only; beer garden and playground where dogs are permitted. Closed on Sunday evenings.

Lunch served 12–2.30; last orders 2pm

Price: lunch £; evening meals ££

B The Glapwell
Bramley Vale
_© (01246) 850264_

An imposing stone-built public house of the 1930s on a busy main road. Hot and cold bar meals. Surrounded by car parking.

There is a play area and dogs are allowed.

Last orders for meals 2.30pm and 10pm every day

Price: ££

▶ _filling station on the road from the junction_

Sheffield (S), Worksop A616 **30**

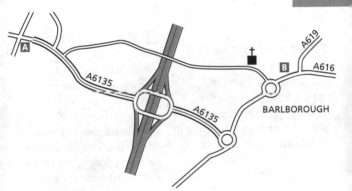

A Blacksmith's Arms
Nr Renishaw
_© (01246) 432180_

A cream-painted pub on the main road. Bar food, children's playground and garden. Open views around; dogs allowed. Parking for Caravan Club members.

Last orders for meals 2.30pm and 10.30pm; open all day Saturday

Price: £

▶ _filling station on the road from the junction_

B De Rodes Arms
Barlborough
_© (01246) 810345_

A modernized crossroads eating house with a full menu which is served all day and every day. Family dining room and no-smoking area.

Open daily from 11.30am (noon on Sunday) to 10pm; food served all day

Price: ££

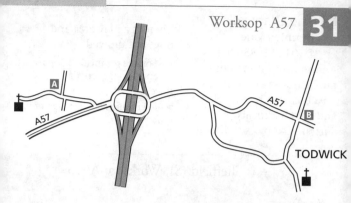

TODWICK

A The Yellow Lion
Aston
☎ (0114) 287 2283

A pleasant cream-painted country pub serving bar food, lunches and evening meals including Sunday all day until 7pm. Outside seating at rear. Provides a playground and family room where dogs are allowed.

Meals daily from midday to 9pm (7pm Sunday)
Price: ££

B The Red Lion
Todwick
☎ (01909) 771654

A mock half-timbered pub, now much enlarged with extensive stone-faced additions to provide 30-room accommodation. Morning coffee, bar snacks, restaurant lunches and evening meals. Children welcomed but not dogs.

Last orders for meals at 2pm and 10pm (9.30pm Sunday)
Price: £££
▶ *filling station nearby*

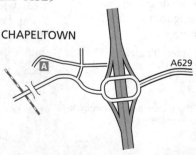

CHAPELTOWN

A The Travellers
Chapeltown
☏ (0114) 246 7870
White-painted and slate-roofed pub surprisingly set in the middle of a wood. Bar menu, lunches and evening meals. Beer garden and outside WCs. Children's playground and family room. No dogs.

Last orders for meals at 2pm and 9pm; no evening meals Sunday and Monday

Price: ££

Wakefield A636 **39**

A The British Oak
Crigglestone
☏ (01924) 275286
A plain cream-painted building. Bar meals at midday and evenings including Sunday. Large beer garden and children's playground. No dogs.

Last orders for meals at 2.15pm and 9pm

Price: ££

▶ filling station on the road rom the junction

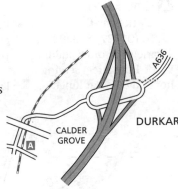

CALDER GROVE

DURKAR

A636

---

41 Morley A650

EAST ARDSLEY

A650

A The Bay Horse
East Ardsley
☏ (01924) 825926
A cream-painted building with added stone frontage. Bar food, lunches and evening meals including Sunday evening with disco. Beer garden. Dogs allowed.

Last orders for meals at 2.15pm and 9.15pm.

Price: ££

▶ filling station nearby

Single junction

The M10 is the short spur leading between the M1 and the city of St Albans.

1   St Albans

A The Falcon
Park Street
© (01727) 873208
A variegated brick building in the high street serving hot and cold bar lunches,

tea and coffee. No children, but well-behaved dogs allowed.

Bar meals available from midday until 2pm
Price: £

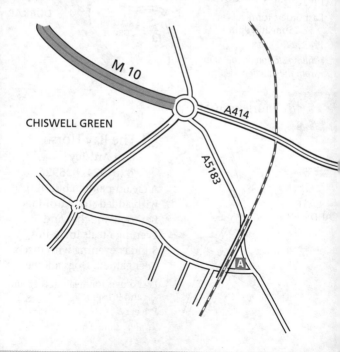

London ◀ ▶Cambridge M11

Junctions 4 to 14

The M11 intersects with the M25 at Junction 6 (Junction 27 on the M25). It passes through the comparatively open countryside around Bishops Stortford, Saffron Walden and the Imperial War Museum for aircraft at Duxford before ending to the northwest of Cambridge.

Junctions 4–6 have no suitable stopping places.

Harlow A414 7

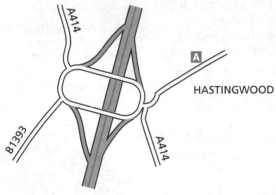

A The Rainbow and Dart
Hastingwood
℡ (01279) 415419

A charming little country pub, said to date from the 15th century. Full bar meals including Sunday evenings. Outside seating in a trim garden but no dogs indoors. Traditional and friendly atmosphere.

Last orders for meals at 2.30pm and 9.30pm
Price: *££–£££*

M11

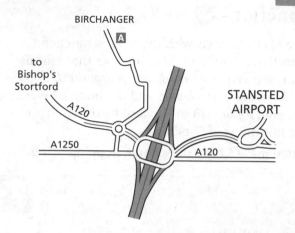

A The Three Willows
Birchanger
✆ (01279) 815913

A quaint cream-painted country pub providing a feeling of well-being. Bar meals at noon and evenings. Small children's playground. No dogs.

Last orders for meals at 2.30pm and 9.30pm daily
▶ *specialities: fresh fish*
Price: ££
▶ *filling station on the road from the junction*

---

9 Newmarket, Norwich A11
restricted access

A Crown House Hotel
Great Chesterford
✆ (01799) 530515

Elegant Georgian house, now a hotel and restaurant. Attractively furnished dining room. Open to non-residents for evening meals on weekdays and all day Sunday. Dogs allowed.

Last orders for weekday evening meals at 9.30pm; Sunday lunches at 2.30pm and evenings 8.30pm
Price: £££

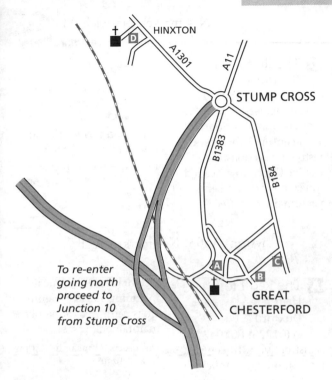

HINXTON

A1301

A11

STUMP CROSS

B1383

B184

To re-enter
going north
proceed to
Junction 10
from Stump Cross

A

B

C

GREAT
CHESTERFORD

B Crown & Thistle
Great Chesterford
(01799) 530278

An attractive cream-coloured village pub with accommodation and displaying traditional East Anglian pargeted plasterwork. Lunch and evening meals except Sunday and Monday nights. Beer garden with playground; dogs allowed.

Last orders for meals at 2pm (2.30pm Sunday) and 9pm Tues–Sat
Price: ££

C The Plough
Great Chesterford
(01799) 530283

Pink-washed village pub with a dining room in a modern extension. Bar meals, family room, playground and beer garden. Dogs allowed.

Last orders for meals at 2pm and 9pm
Price: ££
▶ *this attractive village was once a Roman settlement*

D The Red Lion
Hinxton
© (01799) 530601

A bustling, jettied (overhanging 1st floor) 16th-century inn, recently restored, and boasting George the yellow-headed Amazon parrot and an as yet unnamed stuffed tarantula. Restaurant, bar snacks and outside seating in a well-maintained garden and paddock. No dogs; children outside.

Last orders for meals at 2pm and 10pm (9.30pm Sunday and Monday)
Price: ££

10 Royston A505, Newmarket A11

A The Red Lion Hotel
Duxford
© (01223) 832047

A distinctive 13th-century black and white timbered inn with an immaculate garden and mediæval chapel in the grounds. Accommodation, restaurant and bar meals including Sunday evenings. Dogs permitted. Superbly maintained.

Last orders for meals at 2.30pm and 10pm
Price: £££
▶ *filling station on the road from the junction*

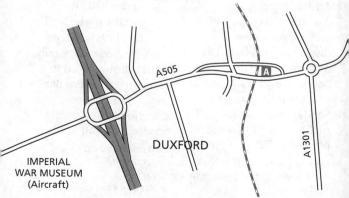

A Old English Gentleman
Harston
© (01223) 870287

A cream-painted inn on a high-street crossroads. Morning coffee, hot and cold bar snacks, lunches and evening meals. Outside seating in the beer garden and children's playground. No dogs indoors.

Last orders for meals at 3pm and 11pm (10.30pm Sunday)

Price: ££

▶ *filling station nearby and on the road from the junction*

12 Cambridge A603

A The White Horse
Barton
© (01223) 262327

A small cream-rendered pub. Morning coffee, lunches and evening bar meals. Outside seating and children's playground. No dogs.

Last orders for meals at 2pm and 9pm

Price: ££

▶ *filling station nearby*

B The Green Man
Grantchester
© (01223) 841178

An old cream-coloured village pub. Serving bar food and summer barbecues. Beer garden beyond the car park. No dogs.

Last orders for meals at 2.30pm and 9pm

Price: ££

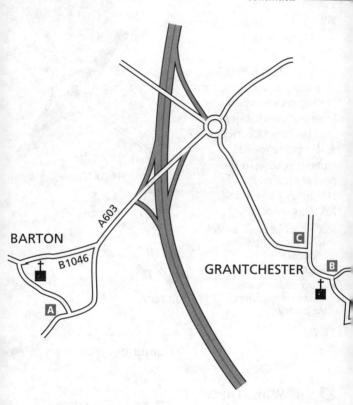

C Rupert Brooke
Grantchester
(01223) 840295

A 19th-century yellow brick pub which is named after the First World War poet who made the town of Grantchester famous. Home-cooked meals as well as tea and coffee are served every day. There is outside seating in a well kept, attractive garden. No dogs allowed.

Last orders for weekday meals at 2pm and 9pm; open on Sundays from midday until 9pm

Price: *£££*

A Three Horse Shoes
Madingley
© (01954) 210221

A white thatched and pargeted pub with a conservatory behind. Restaurant and bar meals are served seven days a week. There is outside seating in a tidy garden. No playground or dogs permitted, but children are allowed.

Last orders for meals at 2pm and 10pm (9pm Sunday)
Price: *££–£££*

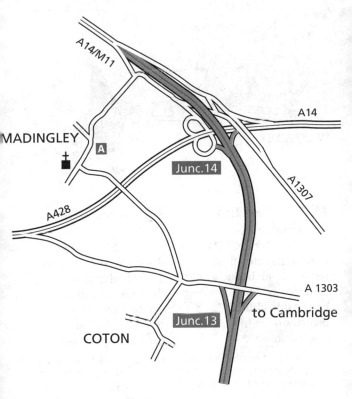

Junctions **1** to **7**

A short motorway linking the M1 to the M62 (east) and the A1(M). For most of its length it runs through the typically flat land of drained marshes. Comparatively lightly used, it allows easy and rapid travel, especially for those going north on the A1.

Junction 2 is the motorway junction with the M1.

Junction 5 is the junction with the M180.

Junction 7 joins the M62 at junction 35.

---

1   Rotherham A631

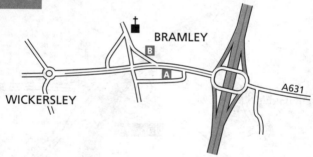

A Travellers Inn
Bramley
✆ (01709) 543924

A stone and cream-rendered pub beside a dual carriageway. There is a beer garden and children's playground behind. No dogs permitted.

Last orders for meals 2.15pm (2.30pm Sundays) and 8pm (closed Saturday evening)
Price: £

B The Sportsman
Bramley
✆ (01709) 543328

A sizeable 1920s mock-Tudor building. Bar food daily except Sunday evening and an outside terrace. On a noisy dual carriageway crossroads.

Food served daily from midday to 4pm; midday to 2pm on Sunday
Price: ££

▶ *filling station on the road from the junction*

A   The John Bull Inn
Waterside
✆ **(01405) 814677**

A 17th-century building which is now the last of seven Waterside pubs on the River Don navigation system. The building has been recently redecorated with cream-coloured rendering. Hot and cold bar meals are available throughout the week. The restaurant serves evening meals and Sunday lunches. This is a thoroughly pleasant and secluded pub. No dogs permitted.

Last orders for meals 2pm (2.30pm on Sunday) and 9.30pm

Price: ££

▶ *filling station on the road from the junction; there are several pubs and restaurants in the old canal town of Thorne*

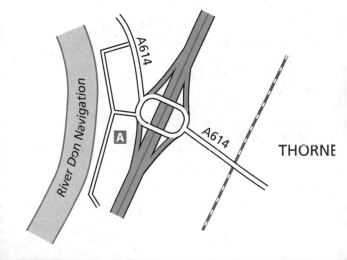

M180

Doncaster ◀
▶Grimsby

Junctions 1 to 5

A short motorway providing easy access from the M18 eastwards, the last 15 miles to Grimsby being dual carriageway. The M181 is merely a short spur to Scunthorpe. The M180 also links up with the Humber Bridge via the A15 dual carriageway. Like the Humber Bridge itself, these roads have always been underemployed.

Junction 3 is the motorway junction with the M181 to Scunthorpe.

Junction 4, Lincoln A15, Scunthorpe A18, is the intersection with the Roman Ermine Street.

---

2 Gainsborough A161

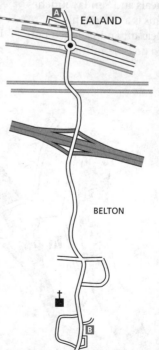

EALAND

BELTON

A The New Trent
Ealand
✆ **(01724) 710315**
An attractive cream-painted pub in Ealand with its canal and river. Hot and cold bar lunches and evening meals except Sunday. Beer garden. Dogs allowed.

Last orders for meals at 2pm and 8pm
Price: £

B Sir Solomon
Belton
© (01427) 873522

A cream-painted and pebbledashed pub in the centre of the village. Hot and cold bar food. Limited car parking.

Lunch served 12–2.30, evening meals Mon–Sat 5–9pm, Sun 5–7.30; last orders half an hour before closing
Price: £
▶ *filling station nearby*

---

5 Humber Bridge, Humber Airport A18
motorway end; dual carriageway continues to Grimsby

A Railway Inn
Barnetby Le Wold
© (01652) 688284

A compact, tidy cream-painted 19th-century pub in the village. Bar lunches and outside seating in a small orchard behind. Dogs allowed.

Last orders for lunch at 2pm
Price: £–££

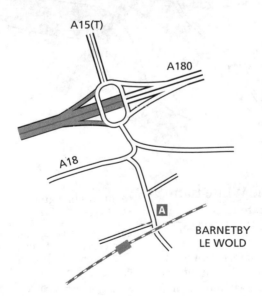

Junctions **1** to **7**

An early motorway, built to connect London to Dover with its Channel ferry services. Although it has never been completed to full motorway status along its whole length, the excellence of connecting dual carriageways leaves little to be desired.

---

2 Rochester, West Malling A228
restricted access

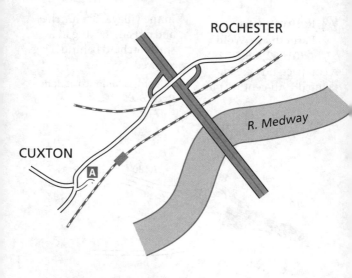

A The White Hart
Cuxton
© (01634) 711857

A cream-painted 19th-century pub, offering bar food. Outside seating on a banked lawn and children's room and playground. No dogs.

Lunch served 12–2.30pm (last orders 2pm); evening meals 7–9.30pm
Price: £
► *filling station opposite*

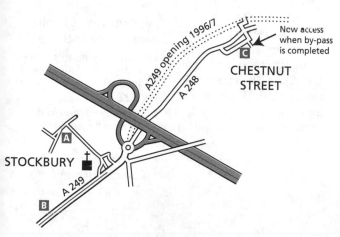

A249 opening 1996/7

New access
when by-pass
is completed

C

**CHESTNUT
STREET**

A 248

A

STOCKBURY †

A 249

B

B The Three Squirrels
Nr Stockbury
℃ **(01795) 842449**

A peach-coloured brick
wayside pub on the dual
carriageway. Coffee,
restaurant and bar meals
with a 'traditional' Sunday
lunch. Beer garden and
children's playground. No
dogs. Difficult to reach
from the north.

Last orders for meals at 2pm
and 10.30pm
Price: ££

▶ *filling station on the road from
junction*

A The Harrow Inn
Stockbury
℃ **(01795) 842546**

A brick-built pub offering
home-cooked food all week
except on Sunday evening.
Small family garden and
children welcomed.
No dogs.

Last orders for meals at 2pm
and 9.30pm (closed Sunday
evening)
Price: £–££

▶ *filling station on the road from
the junction*

C ## The Tudor Rose
Chestnut Street
✆ **(01795) 842575**

A whitewashed pub with a conservatory, at the end of the village. Hemmed between a dual carriageway and a closed off old road. Extensive bar menu and an evening carvery. Family room but no dogs.

Last orders for meals at 2.30pm and 9.30pm daily (10pm Fri and Sat)

Price: ££

▶ *filling stations (two) on the road from the junction*

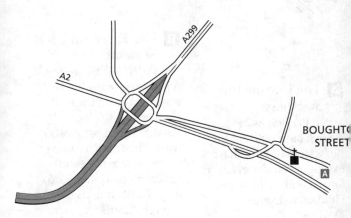

A ## The Queen's Head
Boughton Street
✆ **(01227) 751369**

An old white-rendered house in an attractive village. Morning coffee, lunches and evening meals. Attractive garden. Bed and breakfast. No facilities for children and no dogs.

Last orders for meals at 2pm and 8.30pm; closed for food Sundays

▶ *specialities: fresh fish*

Price: ££

Dartford ◀ ▶Folkestone

Junctions **1** to **13**

A recently completed motorway designed to carry Channel Tunnel traffic on to the main road network via the M25. Much of the Kentish scenery is attractive and the road is well designed to appreciate it.

Motorway junction with M25 (Junction 3) **1**
getting off the motorway is not easy

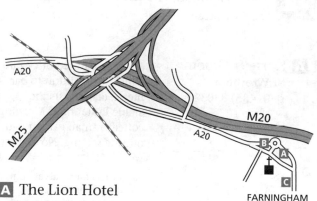

FARNINGHAM

A The Lion Hotel
Farningham
✆ (01322) 866035

An attractive old Georgian coaching inn, now a hotel with restaurant, carvery and bar. Pleasantly located in the village by a small river. Children admitted, outside seating and playground. No dogs indoors.

Last orders for meals at 2.30pm and 10.30pm. Open on for food Sundays midday until 11pm
Price: £££

B The Chequers
Farningham
✆ (01322) 865222

A brick-built pub in the centre of the village. Hot and cold snacks at the bar at lunchtime. No dogs. Parking on the street.

Lunch served Mon–Sat 11am–2pm
▶ *specialities: home-made pies cooked with beer or stout*
Price: £

M20

C The Pied Bull
Farningham
℡ **(01322) 862125**
A white-painted brick building in the village. Hot and cold bar snacks at lunchtime only except

Saturday and Sunday. Beer garden. Dogs allowed.

Lunch served Mon–Fri noon–2pm

Price: £

▶ *filling station in the village*

---

2 Paddock Wood, Gravesend, Tonbridge (A227)
restricted access

A Horse & Groom
Nr Wrotham
℡ **(01435) 830320**

A cream-painted brick pub which, in addition to bar meals, also boasts the Stable Restaurant. Morning coffee, a small garden with outside seating. No dogs at weekends.

Last orders for meals at 2pm and 9.30pm (8.30pm Sunday; restauant closed Tues eves)

Price: ££

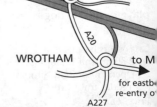

WROTHAM   to M

for eastb
re-entry o

A227

A20

5 Aylesford A20

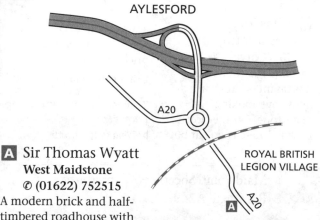

AYLESFORD

A20

ROYAL BRITISH
LEGION VILLAGE

A20

A Sir Thomas Wyatt
West Maidstone
✆ (01622) 752515
A modern brick and half-
timbered roadhouse with
restaurant, family room
and bar. Outside seating
and a large concrete car
park. Clean and efficient.
Dogs allowed.

Last orders for meals at 2.30pm
and 10.30pm daily
Price: **£££**
▶ *filling station nearby*

6 Maidstone, Chatham A229

B

A

A229

MOTEL

SANDLING

A The Lower Bell
Kits Coty
(01634) 861127
A white-rendered old
country pub almost
submerged by a new
crossroads embankment.
Home-cooked meals and
snacks at the bar.

Lunch served daily
11am–3pm; evening meals
6–10pm
Price: £

B Kits Coty Restaurant
Kits Coty
© (01634) 684445

A pleasant ochre-painted house overlooking Maidstone and the North Downs. There is no bar but a smart comfortable restaurant at reasonable prices. No dogs.

Last orders for meals at 2pm and 10pm; closed Saturday lunch and Sunday evenings
Price: £££
▶ *filling station nearby*

---

7 Maidstone, Sheerness, Canterbury, Ramsgate A249

A The Cock Horse
Detling
© (01622) 737092

An old white-rendered and clapboard pub on a corner in this picturesque village. The bar serves home-cooked lunches and evening meals. No dogs.

Last orders for meals at 2.30pm and 9.30pm; open for food all day Sundays
Price: ££

B The Chiltern Hundreds
Penenden Heath
© (01622) 752335

An early Victorian, square-built, yellow brick pub on a roundabout. Modern conservatory and interior decor. Friendly service and bar meals for lunches and suppers. Resident dog, so canine visitors by appointment.

Last orders for meals at 2.30pm (2pm Sunday) and 9pm
▶ *specialities: Sunday lunch roast*
Price: £££

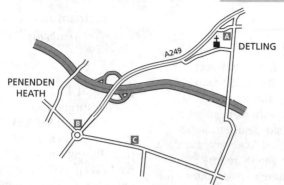

C The Chimneys
Nr Maidstone
© (01622) 734211

An old cream-painted farm house converted to a steak house with bars and restaurant. Morning coffee and afternoon teas served in addition to normal bar meals. Outside seating. No dogs. Open every day.

Last orders for weekday meals at 1.45pm and 9.45; open Sundays from midday until 8.45pm
Price: £££

A Great Danes Hotel
Eyhorne Street
© (01622) 730022

A large modernized cream-painted hotel designed principally for the business community. Look for Rick's Bar for bar and restaurant food.

Children's playground but no dogs.

Last orders for restaurant meals at 2pm and 9.15pm (late nights Friday and Saturday)
Price: £££ in restaurant but £ snacks all day at the bar

M20

B The Windmill
Eyhorne Street
© (01622) 880280

A picturesque old village pub with rear garden and outside seating. Home-cooked food served at the bar. Family room, children's playground and dogs allowed.

Last orders for weekday meals at 3pm and 10pm. Open Sunday from midday until 9.30pm

Price: £££

▶ *filling station on the road from the junction*

C Sugar Loaves
Hollingbourne
© (01622) 880220

A white-painted old village pub offering coffee and bar food except on Sunday. Outside family seating in a small back garden and dogs allowed.

Last orders for meals at 2pm and 9pm (closed Sunday evening)

Price: ££

▶ *filling station nearby*

---

9 Ashford A20, Canterbury (A28)

A Hare & Hounds
Potters Corner
© (01233) 621760

Originally an 18th-century inn, now heavily restored without losing its antiquity, on the busy A30. Reputed for its good food and wines. Beer garden behind. Dogs and children admitted.

Last orders for meals at 2pm and 9.30pm; closed Sunday and Tuesday evenings

Price: ££

A The White Horse
Willesborough Lees
✆ **(01233) 624257**

A small whitewashed pub in the village, serving coffee, home-cooked bar food and dinners. Beer garden. No dogs.

Last orders for meals at 2.30pm and 10pm daily

Price: ££

▶ *filling station on the road from the junction*

B Blacksmith's Arms
Willesborough Lees
✆ **(01233) 623975**

A whitewashed tile-hung village pub. Coffee, snacks, lunches and evening meals; home-made specialities every day. Family garden and children's playground. No dogs.

Last orders for meals at 2.15pm and 9.30pm (9pm Sunday)

Price: £££

▶ *filling station nearby*

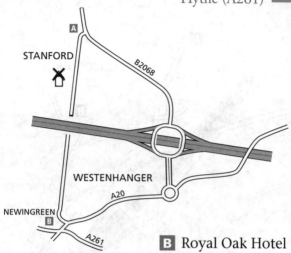
STANFORD

B2068

WESTENHANGER

A20

NEWINGREEN

A261

B Royal Oak Hotel
Newingreen
℗ (01303) 264663

An old apricot-coloured
pub developed into a motel
with restaurant, carvery
and bars. Coffee, lunches
and evening meals all
week. Some outside seating
and play equipment in the
garden. Dogs allowed.
Close to Folkestone
Racecourse.

Last orders for weekday meals
at 3pm and 10pm; open all
day Sundays
Price: *£–££*
▶ *filling station opposite*

A The Drum
Stanford
℗ (01303) 812125

A whitewashed, low-roofed
country pub. Bar meals and
snacks, lunches and
evening meals. Outside
seating in a well-tended
garden with children's
playground. Dogs allowed.

Last orders for meals at 2pm
and 9pm (except Sunday
evening)
Price: *££*
▶ *specialities: Sunday roasts*

13 End of motorway

▶ *There is nothing closer to this junction than Folkestone itself, which
should provide a wide choice of eating places.*

Junctions 9 to 10

A short spur of motorway connecting the M25 to Gatwick International Airport. The numbering of the junctions suggests that this road may one day be extended if the need arises.

Junction 9 is the exit to Gatwick Airport.

Crawley, East Grinstead A264 **10**

COPTHORNE

CRAWLEY

Last orders for meals at 2pm and 10.45pm
Price: £££
▶ *specialities: roast rib of beef*

A Copthorne Hotel
Copthorne
℃ (01342) 714971
A sprawling modern tile-hung brick complex often used as a conference centre. There are full hotel, restaurant and brasserie facilities, and an ornamental garden complete with swans. Reservations are recommended. Children's playground and they are allowed in the brasserie. No dogs in the restaurants.

B Prince Albert
Copthorne Village
℃ (01342) 712702
An unsophisticated semi-urban cream-painted pub. Bar snacks daily and a garden with outside seating. Dogs under control allowed. Tree house for children in large gardens.

Lunch served Mon–Sat noon–2pm; also Fri, Sat night and Sun lunch in summer only
Price: £

M25 London Orbital

Junctions **3** to **31**

The sole purpose of this motorway system is to keep circulating traffic out of the centre of London. It seems to have attracted heavy goods vehicles far in excess of original calculations, particularly with the completion of the Channel Tunnel, and extensive alterations are to be anticipated for some years to come.

A number of motorways start within the perimeter of the M25 but no attempt has been made to list stopping places lying inside, since it is felt that the traveller will either be at the beginning or end of a journey when on them.

Junction numbers start south of the Thames east of London, and build up in a clockwise direction.

Junction 1 and 2 have difficult or no access/exit at the Dartford Tunnel entry and A2 intersection.

Junction 11 to junction 15: mostly motorway junctions. Elsewhere, no attractions.

Junction 21: motorway junction with M1 north, Luton

---

3 London, Maidstone A20, Swanley B2173
not easy to get off the motorway

A The Lion Hotel
Farningham
℡ (01322) 866035
An attractive old Georgian coaching inn, now a hotel with restaurant, carvery and bar. Pleasantly located in the village by a small river. Children admitted, outside seating and playground. No dogs indoors.

Last orders for meals at 2.30pm and 10.30pm. Open on Sundays midday until 11pm
Price: £££

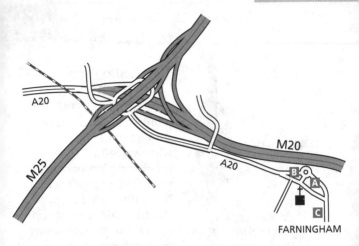

FARNINGHAM

B The Chequers
Farningham
✆ (01322) 865222

A brick-built pub in the centre of the village. Hot and cold snacks at the bar at lunchtime. No dogs. Parking on the street.

Lunch served Mon–Sat
  11am–2pm
▶ *specialities: home-made pies cooked with beer or stout*
Price: £

C The Pied Bull
Farningham
✆ (01322) 862125

A white-painted brick building in the village. Hot and cold bar snacks at lunchtime only except Saturday and Sunday. Beer garden. Dogs allowed.

Lunch served Mon–Fri
  noon–2pm
Price: £
▶ *filling station in the village*

Bromley A21 Orpington A224　**4**

A Badger's Mount
✆ (01959) 534777

1930s style red-brick half-timbered road house. Full menu served all day and families welcomed. Garden with play equipment and orchards behind; no dogs indoors. Some way from the junction.

Open daily from 11.30am
  (midday Sunday) until
  10pm
Price: ££

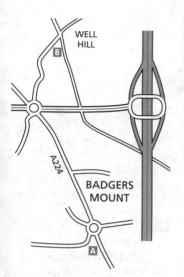

B ## The Bo Peep
Well Hill
✆ **(01959) 534457**
A brick and flint cottage
dating from 1548, with
whitewashed 1710
extension. Non-smoking
restaurant and bar meals.
No facilities for dogs or
children. Outside seating in
the garden and surrounded
by strawberry fields.

Last orders for meals at 2pm
and 9.15pm daily
Price: ££

5 Westerham, Sevenoaks A25

A ## White Horse
Sundridge
✆ **(01959) 562837**
A cream-painted
pebbledashed pub on the
crossroads. Home-
cooked bar food
lunches
and evenings.
Fresh coffee.
Attractive
herbaceous
borders
around the
car park.
Dogs permitted.

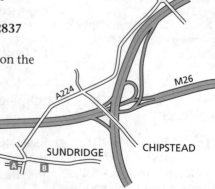

Last orders for meals at 2.30pm
and 9.30pm (9pm Sunday)
Price: ££–£££

B The Lamb
Sundridge
© (01959) 562873
A white-painted brick country pub with extensions. Outside seating in the garden, playground and dogs allowed.

Last orders for meals at 2pm (1.30pm Sunday) and 9.30pm
Price: £

East Grinstead, Eastbourne, Caterham, Godstone A22 **6**

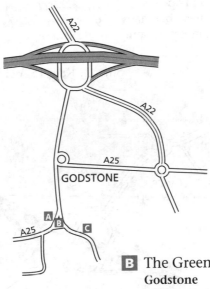

A The Hare & Hounds
Godstone
© (01883) 742296
A tile-hung white-painted building. Home prepared midday and evening meals seven days a week. Small and cosy. No dogs.

Last orders for meals at 3pm and 10pm
Price: ££

B The Green Rooms
Godstone
© (01883) 742288
A pleasant-looking restaurant overlooking a smartly kept green. Comfortable and expensive.

Dinners served Saturday and Sunday evenings only from 7pm to 10pm
▶ *specialities: English country cuisine*
Price: £££; 5-course meal for £25

East Grinstead, Eastbourne,
Caterham, Godstone A22 **6**

continued

C The White Hart
Godstone
℡ (01883) 742521
An impressive tile-hung brick coaching inn. The interior has been much altered to form open bars and eating areas, but many of the old timbers remain.

Wide menu and friendly service. No dogs.

Last orders for meals at 2.30pm and 10.30pm
Price: ££–£££ in restaurant
▶ *filling station on the road from the junction*

Sutton, Reigate A217 **8**

LOWER
KINGSWOOD

A217

QUARRY
HILL

A The Mint Arms
**Lower Kingswood
Reigate**
℡ (01737) 242957
A plain, tile-hung and white-rendered 1930s pub. Hot and cold bar meals, beer garden and barbecues in the summer. Children's playground and dogs allowed in the bar.

Last orders for meals at 3pm and 10pm; open Sundays from noon to 9.30pm
Price: ££
▶ *filling station on the road from the junction*

B Bridge House Hotel and Restaurant
Reigate Hill
© (01737) 246801
A modern hotel with enclosed terraced restaurant. Restaurant and bars open to non-residents. There are fine views over the surrounding countryside. No dogs.

Last orders for meals at 2pm and 10pm (9.30pm Sunday)
Price: £££

▶ *filling station down the hill*

---

9 Leatherhead A243 Dorking A24

A The Star
Leatherhead
© (01372) 843683
A modest-sized cream-coloured country pub with a large car park and beer garden at rear. Bar snacks at midday and Sunday roasts if booked. Playground and family room. No dogs.

Last orders at 2pm
Price: ££

▶ *filling station on the road from the junction*

LEATHERHEAD GOLF CLUB

A244

split junction

A244

ASHTEAD

A Hilton National
Cobham
℡ (0181) 680 3000
Originally an Edwardian
country house with
spacious gardens, now
converted into a hotel
with 168 bedrooms and
two restaurants plus a
carvery. Not for those on a

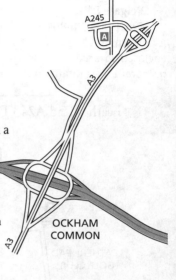

budget. Dogs allowed
under control.

Last orders for meals at 2pm
and 10pm (9.30pm
Sunday)
Price: £££££

17 Maple Cross A412

A The Cross
Maple Cross
℡ (01923) 773266
An old white-painted and
tiled pub on a busy road
opposite an industrial
estate. Bar lunches
all week except Sunday.
Children's play area and
beer garden.
Dogs allowed.

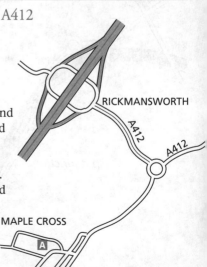

Last lunch orders at 2pm
Price: ££

18 Rickmansworth, Chorley Wood, Amersham A404

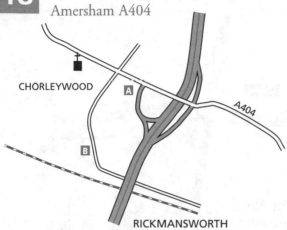

A The Black Horse
Chorleywood Common
℗ (01923) 282252

A little white-painted pub deep in the coutryside. Home-cooked bar meals except on Sunday; outside seating and dogs allowed in the bar. It is amazing how this rural valley has survived the surrounding urban development.

Advisable to book ahead for evening meals.

Last orders for meals at 2.15pm and 9.30pm; closed for food Sundays

Price: £

▶ *filling station on the road from the junction*

B White Horse
Chorleywood
℗ (01923) 282227

An old cream-painted building, lying on the A404 at the edge of the town. Hot and cold bar meals lunches and evenings. Children allowed; no dogs.

Last orders for meals at 2pm and 8.45pm; closed forr food Sundays

Price: ££

▶ *filling station opposite*

M25

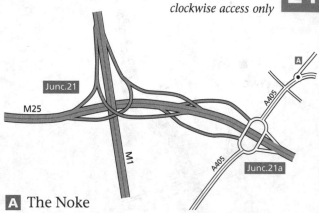

Watford, Harrow A405 & M1 (S) 21a
clockwise access only

A The Noke
Chiswell Green
© **(01727) 854252**

A pleasant, low white-painted building with surrounding garden and trees. Full hotel facilities open to non-residents.

Quiet considering its location. Dogs allowed.

Last orders for meals at 2pm and 9.30pm (9pm Sunday)

Price: £££

▶ *filling station on approach road*

---

22 St Albans A1081

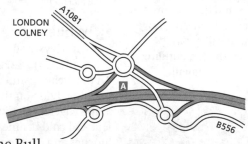

A The Bull
London Colney
© **(01727) 823160**

A white-painted Georgian country pub. Bar lunches, beer garden and children's farmyard. Pizzas served in the evenings. Attractive despite the surrounding road network.

Lunch served daily noon–2.30pm; pizzas in evening, 5.30–11pm

Price: £

25 Enfield, Hertford A10

A Pied Bull
Enfield
✆ **(01992) 710619**

A small whitewashed and tiled country pub of charm now in a built-up area. Home-cooked bar meals. Outside seating in a tidy garden with quiet surroundings. Family room and dogs allowed.

Last orders for meals at 3pm and 9pm except Sunday evenings

Price: ££

▶ *filling station on the road from the junction*

Waltham Abbey, Loughton A121 26

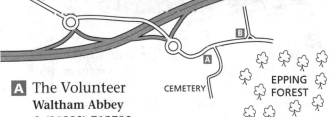

A The Volunteer
Waltham Abbey
✆ **(01992) 713705**

A cream-painted country pub on a busy road but overlooking Epping Forest. Bar snacks with a little outside seating. Family room; dogs allowed in the bar.

Last orders for meals at 2pm and 9.30pm (9pm Sunday)

▶ *specialities: 20 years of Chinese cooking*

Price: £–££

B The Woodbine
Waltham Abbey
✆ **(01992) 713050**

A Victorian brick and tiled building on the same busy A121 looking directly over Epping Forest. Bar snack lunches only. No dogs.

Last orders at 3pm; closed for food Sundays

Price: £

Single Junction

A short but useful motorway that cuts off a corner between the M25 and M20. The single junction is closely linked to Junction 2 of the M20.

1

A The Bull Hotel
Wrotham
✆ (01732) 885522
An attractive old brick coaching inn and hotel in a picturesque village with restaurant and bar meals every day.
Dogs allowed on a lead.

Last orders for meals at 2pm (2.30pm Sunday) and 9.45pm
Price: ££–£££; set meals for £12.50

B The Moat
Nr Wrotham Heath
✆ (01732) 882263
Modern stone and brick-built, tile-hung restaurant and pub beside the busy A20. Children are allowed in the restaurant but no dogs permitted.

Last orders for weekday meals at 2.30pm and 10.30pm; open from midday until 10pm on Sunday
Price: £££
▶ filling station nearby

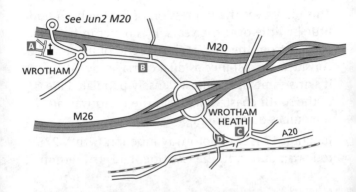

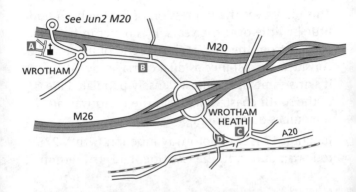 The Vineyard
Wrotham Heath
✆ (01732) 882330

An attractive white-rendered licensed and air-conditioned restaurant with a well tended garden on the A20.
Closed on Monday.
Children welcomed but no dogs allowed.

Last orders for meals at 2.30pm and 10pm (except Sunday evening)

Price: £££

▶ *filling station on the road from the junction*

The Royal Oak
Wrotham Heath
✆ (01732) 884214

A large brick 1930s road house with a Travel Inn behind as an annexe. Comfortable and well organized restaurant and bar meals with a family room. Outside seating by the A20. No dogs.

Last orders for weekday meals at 3pm and 10.30pm; open on Sunday from noon until 10.30pm

Price: £££

▶ *filling station next door*

M27 New Forest ◀ ▶ Portsmouth

Junctions **1** to **12**

This road gives the impression of having been built little by little over the years. It is better in fact than appears from the map and each end of it extends a considerable distance as dual carriageway. Although it skirts some of the most densely populated areas of the south coast views from the motorway are sometimes quite striking.

Junction 12 is the motorway junction with M275 to Portsmouth and the Continental Ferry Terminal.

---

1   Lyndhurst, Cadnam A337

A **Sir John Barleycorn**
Cadnam
✆ ((01703) 812236

A charming and therefore popular long, white-painted thatched row of cottages (with matching outside WCs) said to date from the 12th century. The motorway has closed off the road on which it stands so there is no through traffic. Excellent menu. Ample outside seating but nothing specially for children and no dogs.

Open every weekday from 11am until 10pm; last orders on Sunday at 2.30pm and 9.30pm
▶ *specialities: seafood*
Price: ££–£££

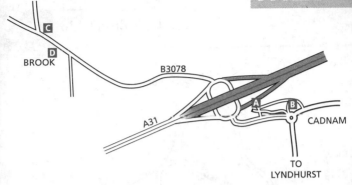

B The White Hart
Cadnam
℡ (01703) 812277

An attractive building in the local style, recently refurbished. Bar lunches and evening meals; children welcomed and dogs allowed on leads.

Last orders for meals at 2pm and 9.30pm (9pm on Sunday)

Price: ££

C The Bell Inn
Brook
℡ (01703) 812214

Based on a fine Georgian house, this three-star hotel concentrates on golf with its own course and club house. The interior is light and open, with a bar with home-made snacks and restaurant open to the public (including children) with full service and expert menus using local seasonal produce available all and every day. No dogs indoors.

Last orders for meals at 2.30pm (2pm Sunday) and 9.30pm (9pm Sunday)

Price: £££

D The Green Dragon
Brook
℡ (01703) 813359

A thatched white-painted old pub of great charm likely to have more horses parked outside than BMWs. Saloon and snug bars offering bar meals or snacks at all times and every day. Large beer garden with children's playground overlooking a paddock. Excellent and friendly service and dogs permitted.

Last orders for meals at 2pm (2.30 Sunday) and 9.30pm (9pm Sunday)

Price: ££; most of the food is home-cooked

▶ *filling station in the village*

Salisbury, Bristol A36 **2**

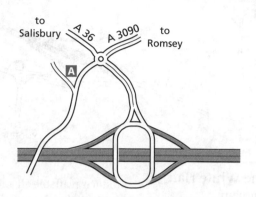

A Heathlands Hotel and the Vine Inn
Wigley
© **(01703) 814333**

A combined hotel and pub based on an 18th-century house; modern additions form the accommodation. The interior of the inn is traditional with bar snacks and meals available. There is outside seating on the asphalt car park. The hotel is comfortable with a smart restaurant and large private garden at the rear. No dogs indoors.

Last orders in the restaurant at 1.45pm and 9.15pm daily
Price: £££

▶ *filling station on the road from the junction*

5 Southampton Airport, Eastleigh A334

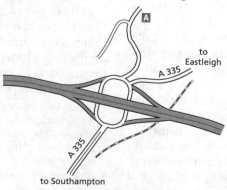

A The Concorde Club
North Stoneham
© (01703) 613989

An attractive group of old ivy-covered buildings. Although a private club, the wine bar is open to the public for lunches and bar snacks. Attractive and fairly expensive. No dogs and no diversions available for children, although they are allowed in.

Last orders for lunch at 2.30pm Mon–Fri only
Price: ££–£££

Southampton East Dock, Hamble A3024 **8**

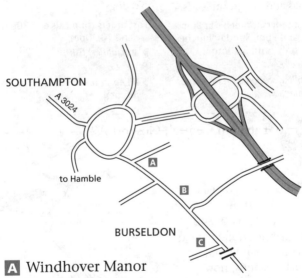

A Windhover Manor
Burseldon
© (01703) 403500

A large modern mock-Tudor country roadhouse set in wooded grounds. Restaurant, bars and outside seating with children's play area. No dogs indoors.

Meals served daily from 11.30am (noon on Sunday) until 10pm in restaurant; bar food 11am–11pm
▶ *specialities: home-cooked specials daily*
Price: ££
▶ *filling station nearby*

B The Crow's Nest
Burseldon
© (01703) 403129

A 19th-century house in a surrounding garden now converted into a comfortable pub with accommodation. Lunches, evening meals and family facilities. Outside seating, children's play area and dogs allowed in on leads.

Last orders for meals at 2pm and 9pm; Sunday lunches only until 2.30pm

Price: £

▸ *filling station on road to the junction*

C Mulligan's Fish Restaurant
Burseldon
© (01703) 403101

Formerly a pub well known to yachtsmen, it is now a large fish restaurant and bar of high standard. Some outside seating and a disabled persons' entrance. No dogs.

Last orders for meals at 2.30pm and 10.30pm

▸ *specialities: fish*

Price: ££

▸ *filling station on road to the junction*

---

11 Fareham Central, Gosport A27

A Roundabout Hotel
Wallington
© (01329) 822542

A large brick hotel named after the roundabout on which it stands, now overshadowed by the new viaduct. Restaurant and bars as well as accommodation. Children welcomed and dogs allowed.

Open daily for food from 11am to 11pm

Price: ££

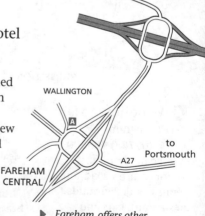

WALLINGTON

to Portsmouth

A27

FAREHAM CENTRAL

▸ *Fareham offers other pubs and restaurants, most notably the Red Lion, a former coaching inn*

Junctions **3** to **12**

Opened in 1995, with the completion of the infamous Twyford Down junction, the full length of the M3 provides a rapid link for commercial and private road-users between Southampton and the London orbital system. It has probably been the subject of more contention than any other road likely to be built in England, though once the scars have healed it may be difficult for future generations to see why.

Guildford, Bracknell A322 (Woking) **3**

A The Cricketers
Bagshot
℡ (01276) 473196

A famous old coaching inn from the days when Bagshot Heath was infested with highwaymen. It maintains its traditions of comfortable accommodation with a restaurant and bars. Meals available seven days a week. Children's playground, no dogs indoors. While awkward to reach from the dual carriageway, it is worth persisting.

Last orders for meals at 2.30pm and 10.30pm (11pm on Sunday)
Price: £££

B The Old Barn
Bagshot
℡ (01276) 476673

Beloved of generations of Officer Cadets from the Military Academy at Sandhurst, the Old Barn (and The Pantiles next door) is still a restaurant and bar, serving bar food (all home cooking) seven days a week. No dogs.

Last orders for meals at 2.30pm and 10.30pm daily
Price: £££
▶ *filling station alongside*

Guildford, Bracknell A322 (Woking) 3
continued

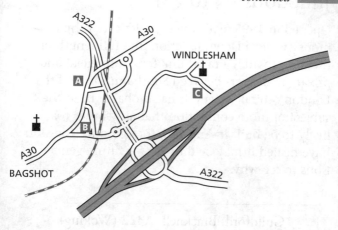

C The Half Moon
Windlesham
℡ (01276) 473329

A pleasant cream-painted gable-ended building on a quiet road. Separate family and public bars. Home-cooked bar food at all times. Large garden with playground behind and a good sense of traditional values. Dogs welcomed.

Last orders for meals at 2.15pm and 9.30pm
Price: ££

4a Farnborough(W) A327, Fleet B3013

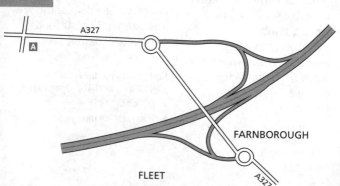

A Crown & Cushion
Yateley
℃ (01252) 545253

On the A327, this is an attractive white-painted country pub set in dense woodland. Restaurant (in the Meade Hall adjoining) and bars. Daily joints and carvery meals. Children admitted but not dogs. Adjoins a cricket ground.

Lunch daily, evening meals Mon–Sat. Last orders for meals at 2pm and 9pm
Price: ££

Farnham A287 **5**

A Dorchester Arms
Hook Common
℃ 901256) 762690

A white-painted pub by the crossroads. Bar meals available at noon and evenings. Outside seating and beer garden. No dogs indoors.

Last orders for meals at 2pm and 9pm.Closed for food Sunday evenings
Price: ££

restaurant and bars. Luncheons and evening meals seven days a week. Children's playground and dogs allowed inside on a lead.

Open for meals daily from 11am to 11pm including Sundays.
▶ *daily specials board*
Price: ££

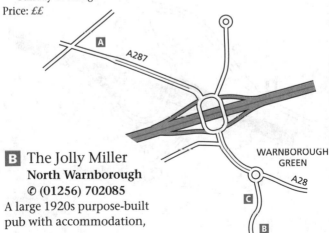

B The Jolly Miller
North Warnborough
℃ (01256) 702085

A large 1920s purpose-built pub with accommodation,

M3

C Blubeckers Mill
House Restaurant
North Warnborough
© (01256) 702953
An attractive rambling old
brick and timber mill
house converted to a
restaurant. Comfortably
appointed with a menu to
match. Large ornate
gardens with a boating
pond (which might once

have been the mill pond).
Reservations desirable,
particularly at weekends.
Children's playground and
family room. No dogs.

Last orders for meals at 1.45pm
and 9.45pm on weekdays;
3pm and 9.45pm on
Sundays.
▶ *specialities: Sunday roast*
Price: ££: weekday set three-
course meals start at about
£10

7 Basingstoke A30 Newbury (A339)

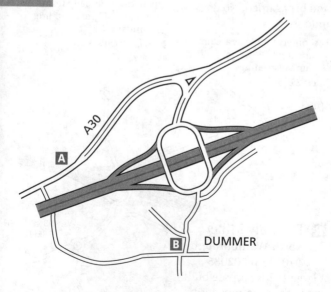

A The Sun Inn
Nr Dummer
© (01256) 397234

A cream-coloured and tiled old country pub by the A30. Restaurant open only Fridays and Saturdays Home-cooked bar meals available for lunches and evenings all week. Playground and dogs allowed.

Last orders for meals at 2.30pm and 10pm daily
Price: ££
▶ *a garden centre adjoins*

B The Queen Inn
Dummer
© (01256) 397367

A secluded and attractive old pub in this charming village. Bar meals including Sunday evenings served at well laid-out partitioned tables. Caters for evidently well-heeled locals. Children's playground. No dogs.

Last orders for meals at 2.30pm and 10pm (9pm on Sunday)
Price: ££

Winchester A34 **9**

▶ *Easy access to Winchester for a variety of eating places.*

Romsey A31 **11**

A The Bridge Hotel
Shawford
© (01962) 713171

A white-painted, dormer- and bow-windowed country pub with accommodation. Lounge and bar meals all week. Pool tables and background music, but comfortable.

Family room and children's playground; no dogs indoors.

Last orders for meals at 2.15pm and 9.30pm (9pm on Sunday)
Price: ££; there are often promotional meals-of-the-day

M3

B The Captain Barnard
Compton
© (01962) 712220

A large, modern cream-painted and pantiled building with a garden and outside seating in front. Restaurant and bar with individual eating areas. Families welcomed and children thoroughly catered for. Good atmosphere.

Food served all day from 11.30am until 10pm

Price: ££

▶ *filling station on the road from the junction*

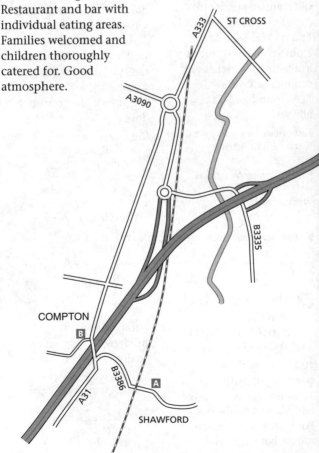

Junctions 5 to 49

One of the earliest built, the M4 passes through a variety of geological areas of England and South Wales. Starting in the Thames Valley, it traverses the Marlborough Downs and drops through the Cotswolds before crossing the River Severn into Wales. After its passage through the industrial heart of South Wales it ends at Carmarthen and becomes dual carriageway to Fishguard and Pembroke.

Between London and the River Severn, the old road network was dense and so there is an unusually large number of stopping places close by the motorway.

As a curious statistic, dogs are more welcome at the hostelries of this motorway than any other.

▶ *Note: to avoid confusion, place names on the M4 in Wales have been given in their English versions only.*

Reading, Basingstoke, Wokingham A33 **11**

A The Wheatsheaf
Grazeley
℗ (01734) 883535
An attractive, small, white-painted country pub on the roadside set in green fields. Bar meals, lunches and evenings except Sunday evening. Family room. Beer garden on both sides and a pleasant layout and situation. Children and dogs allowed.

Last orders for meals at 2pm and 9pm; closed for food Sunday evenings
Price: £££

M4

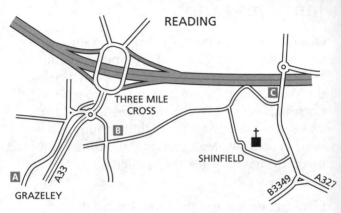

B The Swan
Three Mile Cross
℘ **(01734) 883674**

An old white-painted village pub offering morning coffee, home-cooked bar meals for lunches and evenings in traditional style. Family room and garden but no dogs indoors.

Open weekdays from 11am to 11pm (Sundays noon to 10pm); food served all day
Price: ££

▶ *two filling stations nearby*

C The Black Boy
Shinfield
℘ **(01734) 883116**

A cheerful cream-painted pub by the side of the road into Reading. Bar meals for lunches and evening meals seven days a week. Children's playground and dogs allowed.

Last orders for meals at 2.30pm and 10pm (9.30 on Sunday)
Price: £–££

---

12 Theale, Reading A4

▶ *Junction 12 takes you to Theale, which offers a selection of pubs and inns. Owing to traffic-calming devices it is not recommended for wide vehicles or caravans.*

A Ye Olde Red Lion
Chieveley
℡ (01635) 248379

An attractive half-timbered 18th-century country pub in this equally attractive village. Home-cooked lunches and evening meals in a secluded setting with a children's playground, and dogs are allowed in.

Last orders for meals at 2.30pm and 10pm (9.30pm on Sunday)

Price: ££

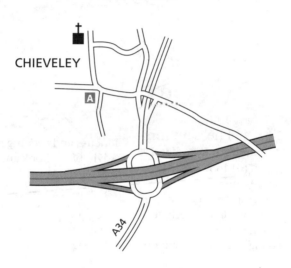

CHIEVELEY

A

A34

A Tally Ho
Hungerford Newtown
℡ (01488) 682312

Turn-of-the-century brick-built pub on the Hungerford road. Lunches and evening bar meals including Sunday. Cheerful atmosphere. No diversions for children and no dogs.

Last orders for meals at 2pm and 9pm

Price: ££

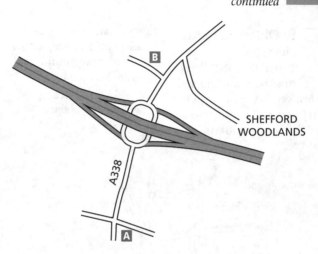

B The Pheasant Inn
Shefford Woodlands
© (01488) 648284

A well-known whitewashed, tile-hung old country pub in a secluded location with a garden. Lounge bar and restaurant; lunches and evening meals. Advisable to book ahead for weekend meals.

Last orders for weekday meals at 2.15pm and 9.30pm; Sunday meals at 2pm and 9pm

Price: **£££**

15 Swindon A419, Marlborough A364

A Plough Inn
Badbury
© (01793) 740342

A cream-washed stone country pub on the Marlborough road. Coffee, bar menu for lunches and evening meals including Sunday. Beer garden and rustic children's play area. Dogs allowed. Good view of the Vale of Swindon below.

Last orders for meals at 2pm and 9.30pm

Price: **££**

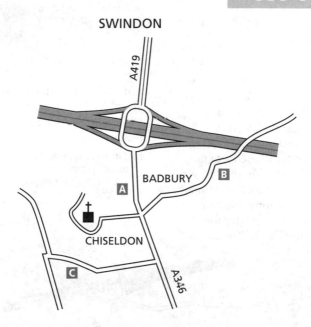

SWINDON

A419

BADBURY

A

B

CHISELDON

C

A346

B The Baker's Arms
Badbury
℡ (01793) 740313

A small cream-painted pub among thatched village cottages. Bar menu for lunches and evening meals including Sunday. Beer garden, family room and children's area; dogs permitted.

Last orders for meals at 2pm (2.30pm on Sunday) and 10pm; closed Mondays and bank holidays
Price: ££–£££
▶ *filling station on the road from the junction*

C The Village Inn
Chiseldon
℡ (01793) 790314

A popular old creeper-covered stone building in the village with some outside seating. Bar meals except on Sunday evenings. Provides a pleasant environment. No dogs.

Last orders for meals at 2pm and 9.30pm; closed for food Sunday evenings
Price: £££
▶ *filling station on the road from the junction*

A Sally Pussey's Inn
Nr Wootton Bassett
© (01793) 852430

This roadside pub presumably takes its singular name from the lantern-jawed woman depicted on the inn sign. There is a well-laid-out bar and informal restaurant. Open every day for morning coffee, bar, restaurant and carvery meals. Beer garden. A well-run establishment; booking ahead is advised. No dogs. Children admitted for meals only.

Last orders for meals at 2pm and 9.45pm; bar meals only on Sunday evenings
Price: **£££**

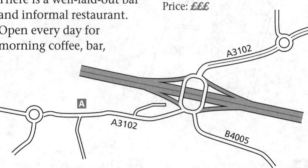

17 Chippenham A350 Cirencester A429

A The Jolly Huntsman Inn
Kington St Michael
© (01249) 750305

A small village pub with accommodation on this attractive village high stre with a small garden behind. Bar and à la carte meals for lunches and evenings 365 days a year and a family room. Cosy atmosphere allowing dogs

Wide variety of Real Ales on offer.

Last orders for meals at 2pm (2.30pm Sunday) and 10pm (9.30pm Sunday)
Price: **££**

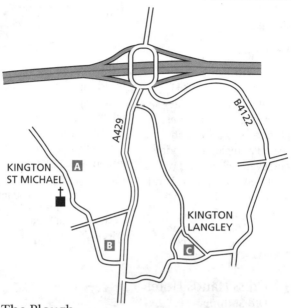

B The Plough
Kington Langley
✆ (01249) 750255

An attractive 18th-century house by the dual carriageway, now a with modern conservatories added and the interior up-dated. Appears to be popular with young business executives from Chippenham. Restaurant and bar meals all week. Some outside seating and a children's playground. No dogs.

Last orders for meals at 2.30pm and 10pm; closed Mondays and bank holidays
Price: *£££*

C The Hit & Miss
Kington Langley
✆ (01249) 758830

A popular and charming 18th-century pub in the middle of this picturesque village. Imaginative bar meals for lunch and evenings. Some outside seating. Traditional welcome includes dogs.

Last orders for meals at 2pm and 10pm; closed Mondays
Price: *£££*

A The Crown Inn
Nr Hinton
☎ (01225) 891231

A traditional Cotswold country pub by an open crossroads on the Bath road. Bar meals at midday and evenings every day. Children's playground and dogs allowed.

Last orders for meals at 2.20pm and 9.30pm; (10pm on Fridays and Saturdays)
Price: ££–£££

B Cross Hands Hotel
Old Sodbury
☎ (01454) 313000

A well-known coaching inn of Cotswold stone. Accommodation, bar meals and restaurant in this very attractive group of buildings. The Queen once had to spend a night here when caught in a Christmas snowstorm. Dogs allowed and corgis encouraged.

Last orders for weekday meals at 2.30pm and 10.30pm (11pm Saturdays); Sundays at 2pm and 10pm
Price: £££

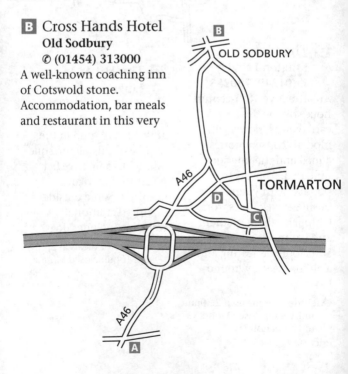

C The Portcullis Inn
Tormarton
℗ (01454) 218263

A creeper-covered stone building in an attractive and quiet village. Accommodation; good bar menu for lunches and evening meals 7 days a week. Pleasant atmosphere, with children and dogs allowed. Large beer garden.

Last orders for meals at 2.45pm and 9.45pm
Price: ££

D The Compass Inn
Tormarton
℗ (01454) 218242

Another creeper-covered group of buildings in open fields. Accommodation of 30 rooms. Restaurant and bars open seven days a week. A popular venue with family room, playground and dogs allowed.

Open daily from 11.30am until 11pm for bar meals; last restaurant orders at 9.30pm
Price: ££

Avonmouth A403 21

A The Boar's Head
Aust
℗ (01454) 632278

A white rough-cast creeper-covered old pub in a quiet village convenient to the motorway. Restaurant and bars for lunches and dinners except Sunday evenings. Outside seating and beer garden but no playground and no dogs.

Last orders for meals at 2pm and 9.30pm; closed for food Sunday evenings
Price: £££

Severn Toll Bridge

River Severn

AUST

A403

A

Chepstow A466 **22**

▶ *Chepstow provides a full range of pubs, inns and restaurants.*

Magor B4245 **23**

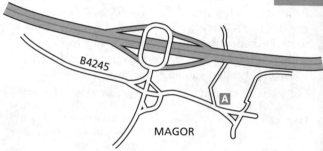

A Wheatsheaf Inn
Magor
© (01633) 880608

Cream-painted rough-cast village inn of good proportions with some en-suite accommodation. The crossroads on which it stands has been bypassed, leaving it pleasantly quiet. Large, informal restaurant and bars, well decorated in local style. Lunches and dinners all week. No dogs.

Last orders for meals at 2.15pm and 9.30pm

Price: ££

▶ *filling station on the road from the junction*

32 Cardiff, Merthyr Tydfil A470

A The Tynant Inn
Morganstown
© (01222) 842313

A delightful and typical low black and white Welsh building with restaurant lounge and bars. Bar menu. Outside seating nearly provides a view of Castle Coch, a splendid example of Victorian romanticism. Worth the effort of finding. Dogs allowed.

Open daily from midday until 9pm. Lunches available until 2.30pm on Sunday; evening meals Thurs, Fri and Sat

Price: £

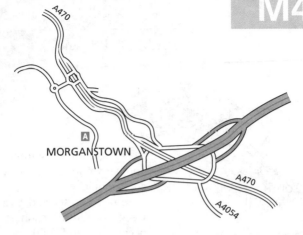

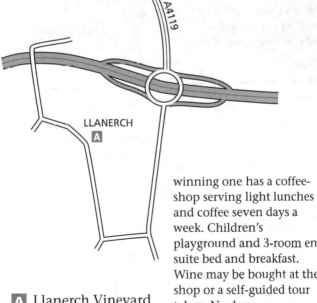

MORGANSTOWN

Llantrisant, Rhondda A4119 **34**

LLANERCH

winning one has a coffee-shop serving light lunches and coffee seven days a week. Children's playground and 3-room en-suite bed and breakfast. Wine may be bought at the shop or a self-guided tour taken. No dogs.

A Llanerch Vineyard
Llanerch
© (01443) 225877
There are few vineyards in Wales and this prize-

Open daily from 10am until 5pm. Not open for evening meals

Price: £

Porthcawl, Pyle A4229

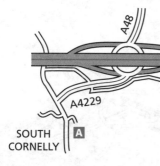

SOUTH CORNELLY

A The Three
Horseshoes
South Cornelly
© **(01656) 740037**
An old cream- and green-
painted pub on a hillside
overlooking a developing

village. Small restaurant
and bar serving home-
cooked lunches and
evening meals seven days a
week. Friendly atmosphere;
beer garden and children's
swings. No dogs.

Last orders for meals at 2pm
(2.30pm Sunday) and
9.30pm (8.45pm Sunday)
Price: £
▶ *filling station on approach
road*

38 Port Talbot A48

MARGAM

A The Abbot's
Kitchen
Margam
© **(01639) 891548**
The Abbey Church of
St Mary's is an exotic
example of ecclesiastical
architecture, originally
dating to 1147. The
Kitchen forms part of the
adjacent Victorian
outbuildings and serves
morning coffee, lunches
and teas seven days a week

in its licensed restaurant.
No dogs. A peaceful oasis at
the foot of a wooded
hillside, out of sight of the
Port Talbot steel works.

† MARGAM
ABBEY

Lunch served
daily
noon–2pm;
morning
coffee and
teas

Price: £–££; 3-course Sunday
lunch under £8
▶ *filling station on the road from
the junction*

London ◀ ▶Birmingham   M40

Junctions 2 to 16

Running close to the A40 as far as Oxford, the M40 then follows the line of the A41 past Banbury and Warwick. It ends with an intersection with the M42 south of Birmingham. It is a particularly useful route for travelling between London or the south coast and Scotland, linking with the M6.

Stokenchurch, West Wycombe A40   5

A Four Horse Shoes
Stokenchurch
✆ (01494) 482265

A pleasant cream-washed and tiled pub on the village green. Morning coffee, bar lunches and evening meals. Small beer garden and children's playground. Karaoke nights Sunday. No dogs. Coaches by prior arrangement.

Last orders for meals at 2.30pm and 10.30pm; no evening meals on Sunday
Price: ££

B Kings Arms Hotel
Stokenchurch
✆ (01494) 483516

A fine large early Georgian coaching inn, with a restaurant, grills and bars. Under new management and currently being renovated. No dogs.

Last orders for meals at 2pm and 9.30pm (9pm on Sundays)
Price: ££

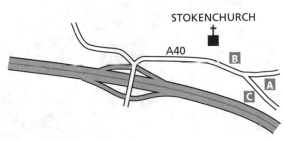

C Fleur de Lis
Stokenchurch
✆ **(01494) 482269**

A white-fronted and ornamentally painted pub standing back from the main road and overlooking the green. Hot and cold bar meals all week. Beer garden where dogs are allowed.

Last orders for meals at 2.30pm and 10.30pm (10pm on Sundays)

Price: £££

▶ *filling station in the village*

Oxford A420 **8**

▶ *Easy access to Oxford with a range of pubs, inns and restaurants.*

6 Wallington, Princes Risborough B4009

A The Leather Bottle
Lewknor
✆ **(01844) 351482**

A charming little white-painted and tiled pub in a rural village. Morning coffee and croissants, bar meals for lunch and dinner including Sunday. Well kept garden in quiet surroundings with playground and dogs Family room. permitted. Recommended.

Last orders for meals at 2pm and 9.30pm

Price: ££

LEWKNOR

10 Northampton A43

A Fox & Hounds
Ardley
℗ **(01869) 346883**

Small white pebbledashed
country pub by the old
main road. Serves
morning coffee and
bar snacks. Beer garden.
A good place to relax
off the motorway.

Lunch served 12.30–2.30pm;
    evening meals
    7.30–9.30pm

Price: *£*

▶ *filling station opposite*

---

12 Gaydon B4451

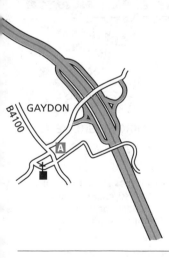

A Gaydon Inn
Gaydon
℗ **(01926) 640388**

An attractive wayside pub;
cream-painted and stone
with tiled roof. Simple bar
snacks including Sunday
evenings. Straightforward
and unpretentious.
Children's playground and
dogs allowed.

Last orders for meals at 2pm
    and 9.30pm

Price: *£–££*

▶ *filling station nearby*

Warwick 15

▶ *Convenient access to Warwick.*

M42 Bromsgrove ◄ ►Tamworth

Junctions **1** to **11**

A motorway designed to keep through-traffic out of central Birmingham by providing a southern bypass. It forms important links with the M1, M4, M40, M5 and M6.

---

1 Bromsgrove A38
restricted access

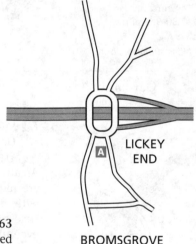

LICKEY
END

BROMSGROVE

A The Forest
Lickey End
✆ (01527) 872063
An old cream-coloured Victorian building now developed into a modern pub with accommodation, restaurant and bars. Meals served include English breakfast. Situated on the elevated roundabout off the dual carriageway.

Last orders for weekday meals at 2.30pm and 9.30pm; Sunday meals from midday until 7.30pm
Price: ££
▶ *filling station nearby*

A Fontana Restaurant
Wythall
℡ (01564) 822824

A white- and green-painted building on the dual carriageway. A reasonably priced Italian restaurant open all week except for Sunday evenings. It can only be approached by looping round the roundabout beyond.

Lunch served Tues–Sun, 12–2pm, evening meals Tues–Sat only, 7–11pm
Price: £££

▶ *filling station nearby*

B Horse & Jockey
Wythall
℡ (01564) 822308

A cream-painted and tiled old pub lying beside and below the dual carriageway. It can only be approached by looping round the roundabout at the end of the dual carriageway and taking the slip road to the left after the Fontana Restaurant.

Lunch served 12–2pm, evening meals 6.30–9.30
Price: ££

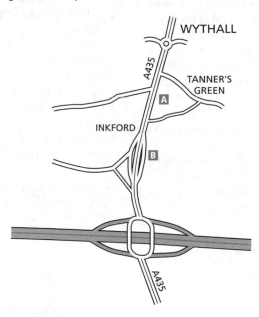

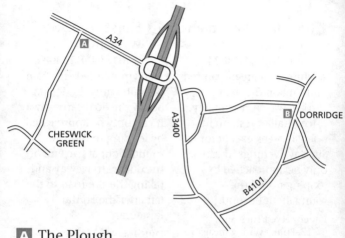

ⓐ The Plough
Shirley
✆ (0121) 7442942

A cream-painted building with shutters and leaded windows. There is a large barn-like restaurant to the rear; bar food and breakfast available to non-residents including Sunday evenings. Accommodation is available at the Travel Inn beyond the car park. Children welcomed, but no playground or dogs.

Open daily from midday until 10.30pm

Price: ££

▶ filling station on the road from the junction at Tesco's supermarket. Two smart restaurants adjoin the Plough

ⓑ Drum & Monkey
Dorridge
✆ (01564) 772242

A cream-painted and slated small country pub on a reasonably quiet road. Extended to provide a restaurant and servery. Beer garden and children's area in a semi-rural setting. No dogs.

Open daily from noon until 9.30pm (10pm Friday and Saturday)

Price: £

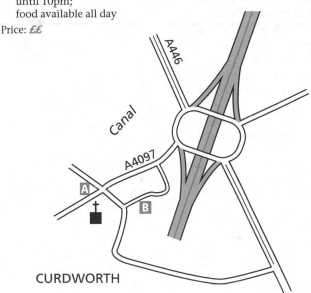

A The White Horse
Curdworth
© (01675) 470227

A cream-painted 19th-century pub on the main road, developed to modern requirements with restaurant and spacious bar areas. Coal fires provide a traditional atmosphere and it is comfortable and well run. Children's playground but no dogs.

Open daily from midday
   until 10pm;
   food available all day
Price: ££

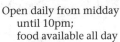

CURDWORTH

B The Beehive
Curdworth Village
© (01675) 470223

A cream-painted and tiled pub in the centre of the old village. Hot and cold bar meals all week including Sunday evenings. Beer garden and children's area to the rear. Attractive and well kept. Dogs allowed.

Open daily from midday until 10pm (9.30pm Sundays)

Price: ££

---

11 Burton (▶N) or Nuneaton (▶S) A444

A The Appleby Inn
Appleby Parva
© (01530) 270463

A large modern pebbledashed inn on the main road. Restaurant and bar meals seven days a week including Sunday evenings. Accommodation wings to the rear and a car park so large it has street lighting.

Open weekdays from noon until 10pm. Last orders for Sunday meals at 2pm and 10pm

Price: ££

▶ *filling station on the road from the junction*

B Black Horse
Appleby Magna
© (01530) 270588

A 17th-century black and white timber-framed building on the old crossroads of a picturesque village in an unspoilt part of England. An interesting old pub. Children and dogs allowed.

Last orders for meals at 2.30pm and 9.30pm; no evening meals on Sunday

Price: ££

▶ *filling station on the road from the junction*

Wolverhampton ◀
▶ **Exeter**

Junctions **1** to **31**

One of the few arterial English motorways that does not gravitate in any way towards London; an unusually high proportion of the M5's traffic is recreational, connecting Birmingham with the southwest resorts.

The number of places where one can get off the motorway for a meal is curiously disappointing, especially in the Vale of Evesham and Malvern Hills, one of the most attractive parts of England. South of Bristol the situation improves in this respect, but almost every junction is now blemished with vast new tin-can warehouses or business parks, seemingly designed to degrade some fine countryside and cause traffic congestion on minor approach roads.

Birmingham (W & Central) A456 **3**

A The Black Horse
Manor Way
Halesowen
☎ **(0121) 550 1465**
A low cream-painted and tiled building on the dual carriageway. Bar meals served at lunch and in the evenings including Sunday.

Surrounded by a car park but offers a cheerful atmosphere. Children's playground; no dogs.

Last orders for meals at 2pm and 9.30pm
Price: ££
▶ *filling station alongside*

B The Black Horse
Illey Lane
℡ (0121) 550 2915

A 17th-century black and white timbered inn with antique interior and restaurant built on. Extensive gardens with horses in attendance and children's playground. Dogs and children welcomed.

Meals from noon until 9.15pm daily (10pm weekends)
Price: ££
▶ *filling station on the road from the junction*

5 Droitwich, Bromsgrove A38

A Robin Hood
Rashwood
℡ (01527) 861224

An old cream pebbledashed pub on the Bury/Droitwich road. The interior has been updated in antique style. Bar meals, lunches and evenings seven days a week. Family room and children's play area but no dogs. Some outside terraced seating; clean and efficient.

Open daily from midday to 9.30pm (10pm on Saturday)
Price: ££

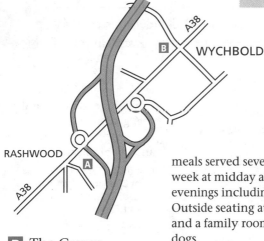

RASHWOOD

WYCHBOLD

A38

B The Crown
Wychbold
✆ **(01527) 861413**
A 1930s mock-Tudor road house on a busy road with restaurant and bars. Bar meals served seven days a week at midday and evenings including Sunday. Outside seating at the rear and a family room. No dogs.

Last orders for meals at 2.30pm and 10pm (9.30pm on Sunday)
Price: £££
▶ *filling station nearby*

6 Worcester (N), Kidderminster A449, Evesham A4538

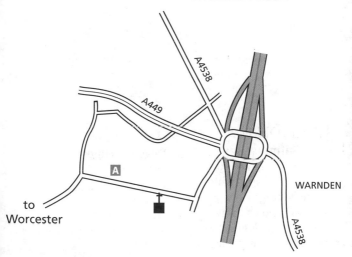

WARNDEN

to Worcester

A449

A4538

A The Poacher's Pocket
Warndon
℃ **(01905) 458615**

An imaginative conversion of an old barn and outlying farm buildings into a roadhouse; the interior has been suitably modernized. Bar meals seven days a week. Large children's playground, car park and beer garden. In the centre of a growing residential and light industrial area.

Last orders for weekday meals at 2pm and 10pm. Open all day Sunday from noon until 9pm

Price: ££

▶ *This junction provides access to Tewkesbury, an interesting old town with hotels and pubs available.*

WHITMINSTER

A The Old Forge
Whitminster
℃ **(01452) 741306**

An old black- and white-timbered forge now serving morning and evening meals. Attractive and well-kept with a rear garden. Dogs and children welcomed.

Last orders for meals at 3pm and 10pm

Price: £–££

▶ *filling station on the road from the junction*

14   Thornbury B4509

A   The Huntsman
Falfield
© **(01454) 260239**
An old cream-painted
roadside pub. Bar meals
at midday and evenings
including Sunday. Outside
seating and beer garden
behind. No dogs indoors.

Last orders for meals at
2.30pm (2pm on Sunday)
and 9.30pm

Price: ££

▶ *filling station nearby*

Bristol, Clifton A4018   17

A   The Fox
Easter Compton
© **(01454) 632220**
A tidily kept cream
and white building
standing back from
the road a little.
Comfortably equipped
and furnished. Bar
meals available seven
days a week; morning
coffee. Family garden.
No dogs in the lounge.

Last orders for meals at
2pm and 9.30pm

Price: ££

▶ *filling station on the road
from the junction*

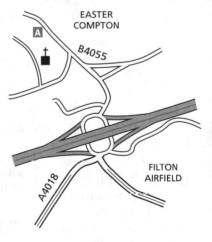

A The Lamplighter
Shirehampton
© (0117) 982 3549

Though difficult, this is a rewarding place to find, overlooking a creek on the far side of the River Avon. Cream-painted Georgian building with iron balustrades, comfortably modernized. Bar meals, lunches and dinners. Pleasant garden surrounded by young lime trees. No dogs indoors.

Last orders for meals at 2.30pm and 9.30pm

Price: £££

▶ *filling station on the road from the junction*

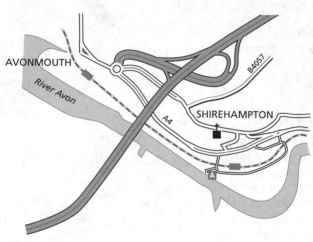

19 Clifton, Portishead A369

A The Rudgleigh Inn
Easton in Gordano
© (01275) 372363

A white-painted roadside pub set conveniently to the junction. Serves coffee, tea, meals and snacks all day. Summer garden and dogs permitted. Relaxing and friendly.

Open weekdays from 11am to 10pm. Last orders on Sunday at 2.30pm and 10pm

Price: ££

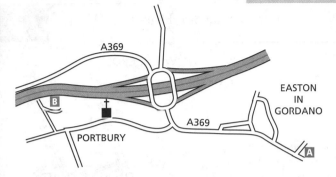

B The Priory
Portbury
© (01275) 372100

A fine white-painted Georgian house now working as a comfortable pub. Hot and cold food, lunchtime and evenings including Sunday. Outside seating in front with a beer garden behind where dogs are allowed. Children welcomed.

Last orders for meals at 2pm and 9.30pm (9pm on Sundays)

Price: ££

▶ *filling station on the road from the junction*

A The Woolpack Inn
St George's
© (01934) 521670

An old white-painted pebbledashed coaching inn where wool used to be packed for local farmers. It is now surrounded by modern housing developments. Restaurant and bar meals including Sundays. Comfortably homely, but book for evening meals in advance. No dogs.

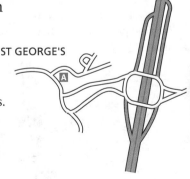

Last orders for meals at 2.30pm and 9.45pm (9.30pm on Sundays)

Price: £££

WHITE CROSS

A The Fox & Goose
Brent Knoll
© (01278) 760223

An attractive 18th-century brick-built coaching inn close by the foot of a Bronze Age hill fort. Bar food, and outside seating. No dogs or coaches.

Last orders for meals at 2pm and 10pm
Price: £££
▶ *filling station adjoining*

23   ### Bridgwater A38 Glastonbury, Wells (A38)

A The Puriton Inn
Puriton
© (01278) 683464

A pleasant-looking cream-painted pantiled pub. Bar meals every day. Clean,

tidy and friendly. Large beer garden. No dogs.

Lunch served between noon and 2pm; dinner from 6.30 to 9.30pm.
▶ *specialities: home-cooked pies*
Price: £–££

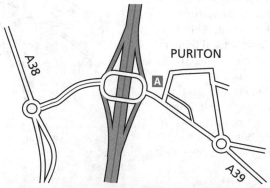

PURITON

A Compass Tavern
North Petherton
© (01278) 662283

A new building on a 17th-century site, attractively executed in old style, cream-and brown-painted. Separate family and bar entrances; very well decorated inside with flagstone floors, beams and divided eating spaces. Imaginative bar lunches and evening meals seven days a week. Comfortable, friendly and well-presented. No dogs.

Last orders for weekday meals at 2.30pm and 10pm. Open on Saturdays and Sundays from noon until 11pm

Price: ££

B The Boat & Anchor Inn
Huntworth
© (01278) 662473

An enticing pub with 4 bedrooms on the banks of the Bridgewater and Taunton Canal (re-opened 1994) arrived at over a Scotch bridge. Long open-plan bars with patio restaurant. Wide and adventurous menu. Meals all day including Sunday. Large canal-side beer garden with playground. Dogs allowed.

Last orders for meals at 2pm and 9pm (9.30pm on Friday and Saturday)

Price: £££

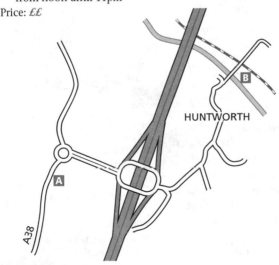

A Blackbrook Tavern
Ruishton
☎ **(01823) 443121**

A cream-painted ivy-covered attractive building close by the junction, with carvery, restaurant and bars. Children's playground but no dogs. Coffee, lunches and evening meals served every day. Deservedly popular.

Last orders for meals at 2pm and 10pm (9.30pm on Sundays)

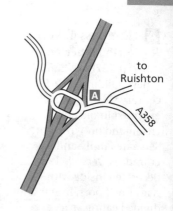

Price: £££
▶ *filling station on the road from the junction*

---

26 Wellington (A38)

WELLINGTON

WEST BUCKLAND

A The Blackbird
Hockholler
☎ **(01823) 461273**

An attractive whitewashed terrace of cottages by the roadside with car park opposite. Accommodation, restaurant and bar snacks including Sunday evenings. Skittle alley and beer garden. Comfortably arranged interior. No dogs indoors.

Last orders for meals at 2pm and 9.30pm (9pm on Sundays)

Price: £££
▶ *garden centre and filling station nearby*

A The Old Cottage Inn
Waterloo Cross
✆ (01884) 840328

A group of modernized buildings providing accommodation for the tourist; grill room with bar styled to 'Olde England' appearance. Good food selection available all week. Families catered for but no dogs.

Open on weekdays from midday until 9.30pm. Last orders on Sundays at 1.45pm and 9.30pm

Price: ££

▶ *filling station nearby*

B The Globe Inn
Sampford Peverell
✆ (01884) 821214

A red sandstone and timbered building on the village street with car park and garden behind. Restaurant and bar meals available midday and evenings including Sunday. Pleasant and friendly atmosphere for the whole family including the dog.

Open daily from midday until 10pm; food served all day

Price: ££

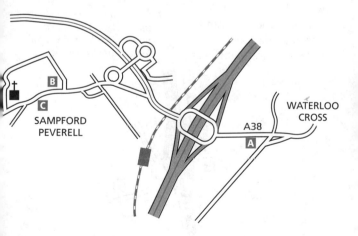

C The Merriemeade
Hotel
Sampford Peverell
℃ **(01884) 820270**

An attractive white
Georgian building on the
village street, now a hotel
open to non-residents.
Restaurant and bars serve
lunches and dinners every day including Sunday
evenings. Large garden and
pétanque at rear. Good
family hotel. Dogs allowed
on leads.

Last orders for meals at 2pm
and 10pm (9.30pm Sunday)
Price: ££ bar snacks; £££ à la
carte
▶ *filling station in village*

28 Cullompton B3181, Honiton A373

A The Weary
Traveller
Cullompton
℃ **(01884) 32317**

A red-brick Georgian inn at
the entrance to the village
with a large beer garden
and playground behind.
Accommodation,
restaurant and public bar; lunches and evening meals
including Sundays. No
dogs.

Last orders for meals at 2pm
and 9.30pm (9pm on
Sundays)
Price: £££
▶ *filling station on the road from
the junction. There are a
number of other pubs in this
large, attractive village*

CULLOMPTON

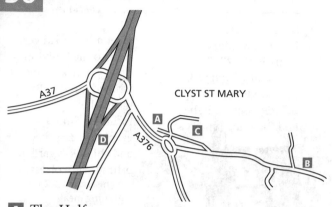

CLYST ST MARY

A The Half Moon Inn
Clyst St Mary
℃ **(01392) 873515**

A cream- and dark blue-painted old pub on the former village crossroads, now largely closed off to passing traffic. Bed and breakfast. Full bar menu with daily specials, including Sunday evenings. Pleasant, traditional layout and good atmosphere. Dogs allowed.

Last orders for meals at 2pm and 9.30pm every day
Price: ££

▶ *filling station on the road from the junction*

B Cat & Fiddle
Nr Clyst St Mary
℃ **(01392) 873317**

A former small wayside pub developed into a popular American-style roadhouse, with pool tables, fruit machines and background music. Self-served meals at the carvery seven days a week. A little outside seating on a patio by a vast and dusty car park. No dogs indoors.

Last orders for meals at 2pm and 10pm every day
Price: ££

▶ *filling station on the road from the junction*

C The Maltsters
Clyst St Mary
℃ **(01392) 873445**

An early Victorian pale green-painted pub on the old high street. Bar lunches every day and dogs permitted.

Last orders for lunch at 2pm
Price: ££

D Blue Bell Inn
Nr Clyst St Mary
© (01392) 877678
A delightful and well preserved cream-painted, pebbledash and thatched inn on a quiet minor road very close to the junction. Appropriate and low-beamed interior. Bar meals all week including Sunday evenings. Large beer and children's garden behind. Very pleasant.

Lunch served 12–2pm;
evening meals
6.30–9.30pm
Price: ££

A Gissons Arms
Kennford
© (01392) 832444
Off the Torquay/Plymouth A38 dual carriageway extension of the motorway; this white-painted

old building has been extensively and well converted into a restaurant with a small bar; heavy panelling and tapestries give an expensive atmosphere. Limited accommodation with 6 bedrooms. All orders for meals taken at the carvery with table service to inside and outside seats. Efficient, friendly, comprehensive service from dawn to dusk. No dogs indoors.

Open daily from 8am until 10pm
Price: £££
▶ *filling station nearby*

Ross on Wye ◀ ▶Tewkesbury

Junctions **1** to **4**

This motorway connects the M5 and industrial Midlands to South Wales, continuing from Ross as a dual carriageway to Newport and the M4, or Abergavenny and the Brecon Beacons. Short as it is, there are some places worth stopping at.

Worcester, Tewkesbury A38 **1**

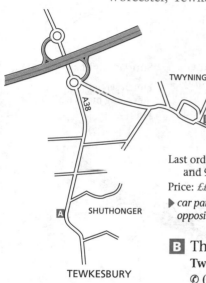

Last orders for meals at 2pm and 9.30pm

Price: ££

▶ *car park and filling station opposite*

B The Village Inn
Twyning
✆ **(01684) 293500**

A group of old cream-coloured buildings with low tiled roofs on the village green. The bar serves lunches and evening meals including Sunday. A good traditional atmosphere.

Lunch served noon–2.30pm, evening meals 6–11pm

Price: £

A The Crown at Shuthonger
Shuthonger
✆ **(01684) 293714**

A small white-painted house by the side of the Tewkesbury road, now a small restaurant with bar meals, lunches and evenings including Sunday.

M50

2 Gloucester A417, Hereford A438

A Rose & Crown
Playley Green
☎ (01531) 650234

An old cream building which could once have been a coaching stop, but is now an attractive and isolated pub on the Gloucester road. The red-brick addition was either a school or village hall and now serves as the restaurant; good bar food in addition except for Sunday nights; congenial.

Lunch served 11am–2pm; evening meals 6.30–9.15
Price: £

3 Gwent B4211

B4211

GORSLEY

A Roadmaker Inn
Gorsley
☎ (01989) 720352

A stone-built house dating from 1847. Hot meals at lunchtimes and evenings in the bar or small restaurant. Genuine home cooking and convivial atmosphere.

Lunch served 11.30–2pm; evening meals 6.30–9; no food available Sunday or Monday nights
Price: ££

Birkenhead ◀

▶Chester M53

Junctions 1 to 12

The northern end of this motorway must be one of the dreariest in Europe, passing through industrial flatlands, refineries and the oil storage facilities of Ellesmere Port. Once into the Wirral things improve, as it passes through well wooded agricultural land.

Birkenhead A552 **3**

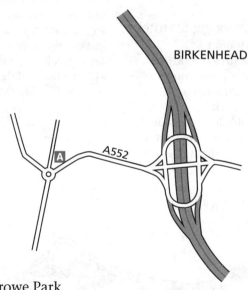

A Arrowe Park
Birkenhead
✆ (0151) 6775031
A large 1930s-style roadhouse. Only midday meals available, at very reasonable prices.

No playground or dogs
Lunch served noon–2pm
Price: £
▶ *filling station nearby*

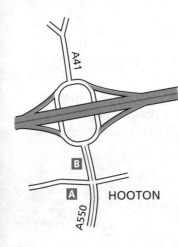

Last orders for meals at 2pm
and 9.30pm

Price: £££

▶ *filling station nearby*

B Chimneys
Hooton
☏ (0151) 3273505

A large Victorian
merchant's house
converted to a restaurant
and bar with limited
accommodation. Lunches
and evening meals seven
days a week. Large garden
with outside seating. No
facilities for children or
dogs.

Last orders for meals at 2.30pm
and 9.30pm

Price: £££

A Woodecote Hotel
Hooton
☏ (0151) 3271542

A 1900s house converted
into a 20-room hotel.
Lunches and evening meals
available to non-residents,
except Sunday evenings.
Dogs just about tolerated.

7 Overpool

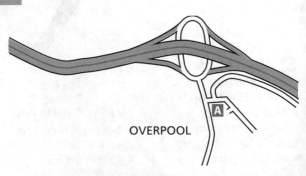

A The Foxfields Inn
Overpool
✆ (0151) 3550200

A modern eating house offering food and traditional beers. Adjacent to fields but with an industrial outlook.

Children's playground but no dogs.

Last orders for midday meals at 2.30pm. Opcn for evening meals on Thursday, Friday and Saturday only until 8.30pm

Price: ££

---

9 East Port Centre, Boat Museum A5032

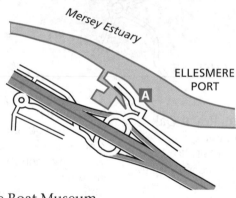

A The Boat Museum
Ellesmere Port
✆ (0151) 3555017

The museum contains an interesting collection of canal and harbour vessels, mostly afloat, in the 19th-century dock complex. Specialist displays are well presented in various listed Georgian and Victorian workshops, warehouses and sail lofts. There are two cafés for snacks or meals. Well worth visiting.

Cafés open daily 10am–5pm April–Oct; 11am to 4pm Nov–March

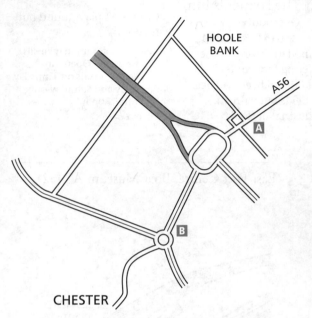

HOOLE
BANK

A56

A

B

CHESTER

B Hoole Hall Hotel
Chester
✆ (01244) 350011
Conventional 3-star hotel,
originally a country house
in its own grounds with
children's playground and
dogs allowed. Restaurant
and bar meals seven days a
week.

Last orders for meals at 2.30pm
and 9.45pm (9pm Sunday)
Price: £££

▶ *Chester abounds in inns, pubs
and restaurants, some of high
quality and considerable
historic interest*

A The Royal Oak
Chester
✆ (01244) 301391
On the approach road to
central Chester, this is a
white 1930s-style half-
rendered roadhouse with
adjoining hotel
accommodation. Lounge
bar, snacks and light meals.
Beer garden at the rear with
children's area. Dogs
permitted.

Last orders for meals at 2pm
and 10pm
Price: £££

Birmingham ◀ ▶Telford **M54**

Junctions **1** to **7**

A modest length of motorway linking the north of Birmingham with North Wales via Shrewsbury. It passes through some pleasant if unmemorable countryside.

Cannock A460 **1**

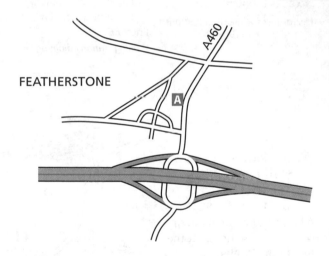

A Red, White & Blue
Featherstone
℡ (01902) 734105
A 1930s black and white roadside pub. Hot and cold bar meals. Outside seating on the road frontage and behind. Children's playground but no dogs indoors. Thoroughly functional.

Last orders for weekday meals at 2pm and 8.30pm; no food available Sundays

Price: £

▶ *filling station nearby*

M54

A Bell Inn
Tong Norton
✆ (01952) 850210

A 19th-century brick-built pub adjoining some very fine earlier sandstone stables. Bar meals available lunches and evenings seven days a week. Beer garden. Large asphalt car park in front with an interesting old milestone obelisk. No dogs indoors.

Last orders for meals at 2.30pm and 9.30pm (9pm on Sunday); late closing (10pm) on Friday and Saturday

Price: ££

▶ *filling station adjoining*

7 Wellington B5061

A Buckatree Hall Hotel
The Wrekin
✆ (01952) 641821

A black and white modern country house hotel. At the foot of the Wrekin, it has a fine view over the Shropshire Plain. Restaurant open to non-residents. Do not be deterred by its rather formal appearance; reservations are probably advisable. Dogs admitted.

Last orders for weekday meals at 1.45pm and 9.45pm; 2pm and 9pm on Sundays

Price: ££; 3-course meals for around £10

▶ *filling station on the road from the junction*

Preston ◀

▶Blackpool   M55

Junctions **1** to **4**

This motorway connects the famous holiday town of Blackpool to the M6. The countryside is green but flat and not particularly interesting and neither are the places where one might stop.

Junction 4 is the end of the motorway.

Garstang A6   **1**

A Taverne Fayre
Broughton
℡ (01772) 866066
Opened in 1994, this is a large roadhouse with all the expected facilities for meals and children's entertainment. Dogs prohibited.

Last orders for weekday meals at 2pm and 10pm. Open all day Sundays from noon to 10pm
Price: ££

Kirkham, Fleetwood A585   **3**

A The Blue Anchor
Fylde
℡ (01253) 836283
A 1930s rough-cast pub described as a 'village inn and eating house', with a carvery, buffet, children's playground and beer garden. No dogs.

Last orders for weekday meals at 2.30pm and 9.30pm. Open from noon to 8.30pm Sundays

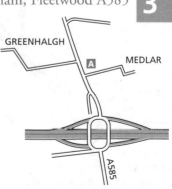

Price: £
▶ *filling station nearby*

Junctions **1** to **16**

This motorway starts with a complicated junction to the M63 orbital motorway round Manchester. For the first few junctions a cool head is required and leaving the motorway remains extremely complex, except for the spur to Manchester International Airport. Free of towns and suburbs, the road runs through pleasant Cheshire countryside then along the industrial salt-flats of the Mersey Estuary. Before ending in green fields, it crosses the southern end of the M53 headed for Chester.

---

6 Wilmslow, Macclesfield, Hale A538

A The Romper
Hale
℗ (0161) 980 6806

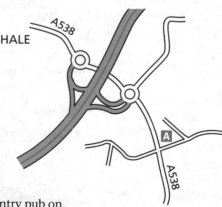

A peaceful country pub on the now disused Wilmslow old road, by the perimeter of the airport. Bar meals at midday only. An attractive beer garden. No dogs.

Open from 11.30am to 11pm Monday to Friday; last orders 3pm and 11pm Saturday and 3pm and 10.30pm Sunday
Price: £

M56

7 Motorway spur to A56
restricted access—rejoin the motorway at Junction 8.

A Nag's Head
Hale
℗ (01565) 830486

This was once a pebbledashed black and white country pub, now extensively renovated and extended.
The interior matches the copper lamp standards in the large car park. Children room and play area. Beer garden and extensive grounds.

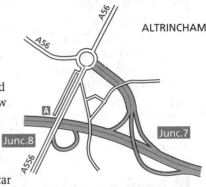

Open daily from 11.00am until 10pm
Price: ££

10 Northwich, Warrington A559

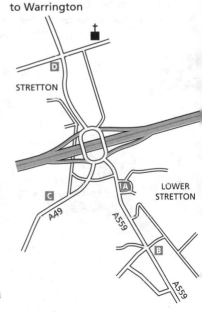

A Ring O'Bells
Lower Stretton
℗ (01925) 730556

A country pub in largely original condition.
No coaches or children but despite this it offers a friendly local atmosphere.
Bar snacks served at tables, some of which are made from sewing machine treadles.

Last orders at 3pm
Price: ££, for a limited menu

B Birch & Bottle
Nr Northwich
℗ (01925) 730225

A rough-cast cream country pub with restaurant in the conservatory. Lunch, supper and cold bar food on offer seven days a week.

Last orders for meals at 2.30pm and 9.30pm

Price: ££

C The Hollow Tree
Lower Stretton
℗ (01925) 730733

Once a private Georgian house converted into a restaurant serving midday and evening meals seven days a week. Separate family entrance, large garden and playground, dogs permitted outside.

Last orders for meals at 2.30pm and 10pm

Price: ££

▶ *filling station on the road from the junction*

D Cat & Lion
Stretton
℗ (01925) 730451

A 19th-century red sandstone building opposite the church converted into a typical modern village pub. Hot and cold meals for lunch and dinner; families welcomed. Accommodation available. No dogs.

Open daily from midday to 9.30pm

Price: ££

11 Preston Brook, Daresbury A56

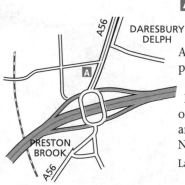

A The Red Lion
Nr Preston Brook
℗ (01928) 701174

A large rendered white-painted road house with limited accommodation. Hot and cold lunches only, children's playground and beer garden. No dogs inside.

Last orders at 2pm. No meals on Saturdays

Price: ££

Liverpool ◀
▶ Huyton & Maghull

Junctions **1** to **7**

Apart from helping race-goers on their way to
Aintree for the Grand National, this is an urban
business motorway. Except for the Safari Park at
Knowsley there are few temptations to leave.

St Helens A580 **4/5**

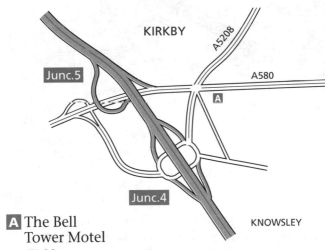

A The Bell
   Tower Motel
   Kirkby
   © (0151) 549 2222

A large pink construction
with accommodation,
restaurant, bars, and
conference facilities. Open
seven days a week except
for Saturday lunch. Lies on
the intersection of two
busy dual carriageways
with restricted access.
Family room but no dogs.

Last orders for meals 2.30pm
   and 9.30pm

Price: £££

▶ *filling station nearby*

M58 Liverpool ◀ ▶Wigan

Junctions 1 to 5

A short inter-urban motorway linking Liverpool to the M6 and Wigan. The countryside is unremarkable but there are places where it is possible to stop and eat.

1 Kirkby, Maghull A506
restricted access

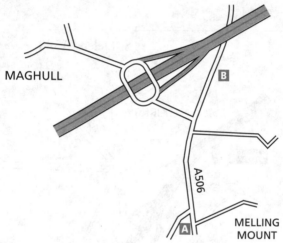

A The Hen & Chickens
Maghull
✆ (0151) 526 3172

A black and white painted country pub with beer garden, playground and family room. No dogs. Hot and cold home-cooked food.

Last orders for meals 2.15pm and 9pm

Price: ££

▶ *filling station opposite*

B Pear Tree
Maghull
✆ (0151) 548 6657

An old cream-painted rough-cast pub at a crossrounds surrounded by an asphalt car park. Bar lunches daily. Children for meals only and no dogs. Daily specials.

Lunch served 12.30–2pm

Price: £

▶ *filling station opposite.*

3 St Helens, Ormskirk A570

A The Stanley Gate Inn
Bickerstaff
℡ (01695) 27700

An old white pebbledashed building offering all-day food and drink seven days a week. Children's playground; dogs barred.

Open daily from 11am to 11pm (10.30pm Sunday)

Price: ££

▶ *filling station on the road to the junction*

B The Blubayou Restaurant
Skelmersdale
℡ (01695) 722970

A modern clapboard building on the dual carriageway with a lane behind in pleasant wooded countryside. It serves lunches and dinners and offers international cuisine.

Lunch served noon–2pm, evening meals 6–10.30 (last orders 1.45 and 10pm)

Price: ££–£££

---

5 Pimbo, Skelmersdale (E) A577

A Lancashire Manor Hotel
Up Holland
℡ (01695) 720401

Once a stone farmhouse and outbuildings, this has been changed by a major programme of extension and alteration into an executive-style hotel with 55 bedrooms, restaurant and carvery. Bar food and barbecues on offer. Facing an industrial estate, with children's playground.

Dogs allowed.

Last orders for meals at 2pm and 9.30pm (9pm Sundays)

Price: £

Junctions 1 to 42

Perhaps no other motorway in Great Britain passes through so varied a range of scenery as the M6. Starting in the pastures between Rugby and Birmingham, it passes through the industrial Midlands to the farmlands of Cheshire before reaching the Manchester Ship Canal and the levels between Manchester and Liverpool. At Lancaster the road rises into the Lake District and over Shap Fell to Carlisle, past hillsides marked by ancient field patterns. North of Carlisle the M6 links up with the A74(M), itself being upgraded to motorway standard, for rapid transit to and from Glasgow and the Scottish motorway system.

---

1   Lutterworth, Rugby A426

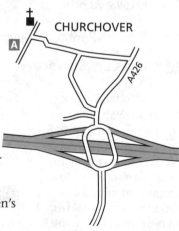

CHURCHOVER

A The Haywaggon
Churchover
℗ (01788) 832307

A white-painted 1930s house with recent stone-faced addition. Large dining areas with a comfortable bar. Children's playground and arcade games room but no dogs allowed. Hard to find as it is tucked away in a picturesque village.

Last orders for meals at 2pm and 10pm (closed Sunday evening)
Price: £££

11 Wolverhampton, Cannock A460, Telford (M54)

A The Wheatsheaf
Laney Green
℡ (01922) 412304

An old brick-built pub with modern additions on the main road. A plain establishment serving bar food.
Dogs permitted.

Last orders for meals at 2pm and 8.30pm; closed for food Sunday evenings
Price: ££

B The Elms
Shareshill
℡ (01922) 52352

An attractive white-painted Georgian house with a modern extension, used as a restaurant with home cooking. Large garden and playground. No dogs indoors.

Last orders at 2.30pm and 9.30pm
Price: £

▶ filling station on the road from the junction

Cannock, North Wales A5 12

A The Spread Eagle
Gailey
✆ **(01902) 790212**
A 1930s-style brick building on a roundabout. Restaurant and lounge bar serving lunches and evening meals including Sunday evening. Car parking on two sides and a beer garden and playground. Children welcomed; no dogs in the garden. Garden centre next door.

Last orders for weekday meals at 2.30pm and 10pm; open Sundays from midday until 2pm
Price: ££
▶ *filling station on the road from the junction*

15 Stoke on Trent, Stowe, Eccleshall A500

A Hanchurch Manor Hotel
Hanchurch
✆ **(01782) 643030**
A very fine 17th-century building with later additions in beautifully maintained grounds with a lake. At present (1995–6) offering a very comfortable 4-room bed, breakfast and residents' dinner service only, pending planning decisions for the motorway.

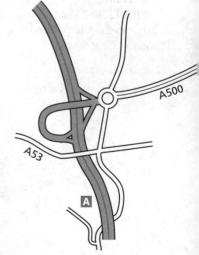

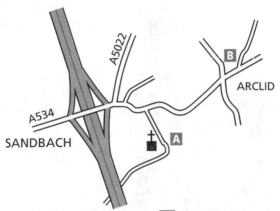

B Rose & Crown
Arclid
℡ **(01477) 500543**

A cream-painted pub on a crossroads. Tea and coffee, bar meals, snacks and a children's menu on offer every day at this cheerful pub. Beer garden. No dogs.

Last orders for meals at 3pm and 9.45pm

Price: ££

▶ *filling station nearby*

A Chimney House Hotel
Sandbach
℡ **(01270) 764141**

A 19th-century house that has been greatly extended to form a country club-type hotel, with spacious grounds and large car park. Meals available to non-residents in the restaurant but these will probably not suit those in a hurry. No dogs.

Last orders for meals at 2pm and 10pm (9.30pm on Sundays)

Price: ££££

▶ *filling station on the road from the junction*

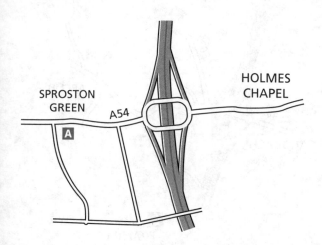

A The Fox & Hounds
Sproston Green
✆ (01606) 832303

A black and white 17th-century roadside pub. Flagstoned bar and restaurant with open beams. Pleasant, friendly and convenient for the motorway. No dogs.

Last orders for meals at 2.15pm and 9pm daily (except Sunday evenings)

Price: £–££

▶ *filling station on the road from the junction*

19 Knutsford A5033 Northwich A54

A The Windmill
✆ (01565) 634162

A sprawling cream-painted rough-cast pub with 3 bedrooms on the junction roundabout, surrounded by a large car park. Bar meals every day and all day. Coaches and dogs not welcomed.

Last orders for meals at 2pm and 9.30pm (9pm on Sunday and Monday)

Price: £££

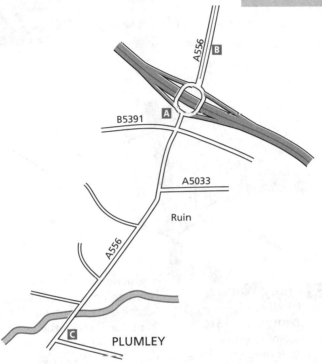

C The Smoker
Plumley
© (01565) 722338

A 16th-century restaurant and inn of local repute named, like the nearby brook, after an 18th-century racehorse belonging to the local nabob. Children's playground and family room. No dogs.

Last orders for meals at 2.30pm and 10pm every day
Price: £££

▶ *filling station nearby. Care needed when leaving the car park to join the A556*

B The Old Vicarage
© (01565) 652221

A large many-gabled building opposite the Windmill, with an ample garden. Now a residential guest-house with 4 rooms serving light lunches, coffee and afternoon teas to non-residents.

Open daily for food from 10am (noon on Monday and Wednesday) until 5pm
Price: ££

▶ *filling station on the roundabout*

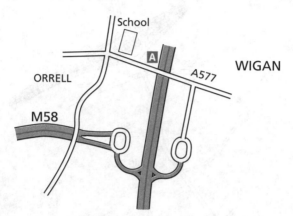

A Priory Wood
Orrell
© (01942) 211516

An elegant Georgian mansion with a wooded coombe to the rear. New 40-room Travel Inn adjacent. Full restaurant and bar amenities every day, noon and evenings. Children's playground behind and car park in front. Facilities for the disabled and babies.

Open daily from midday to 10.30pm; bar food all day, restaurant until 3pm

Price: £–£££

▶ *filling station nearby*

---

27 Wigan, Parbold B5209

A The Dicconson Arms
Nr Standish
© (01257) 252733

Once a small pub but now enlarged to create a lounge bar and restaurant open all week. Situated on a busy crossroads but with some outside seating. Beer garden at rear. No dogs.

Open daily from midday to 10pm (9.30pm Sundays) Last orders 2pm and 9.30pm (9pm Sun)

Price: £–£££

▶ *filling station nearby*

B The Tudor Inn
Wrightington
℡ (01257) 424143

An old stone-built pub serving hot and cold food at lunch and supper, all home-cooked. Beer garden and play area at rear, with an entrance for the disabled. No dogs.

Last orders for weekday meals 2pm and 9.30pm
Open Sundays from midday to 8.30pm
Price: ££
▶ *filling station nearby*

C Charnley Arms
Standish
℡ (01257) 424619

An expensively built new roadhouse. Restaurant with home cooking all week. Children's playground and family dining entrance. No dogs.

Open from midday to 10pm daily (9pm Sundays)
Price: ££
▶ *filling station nearby*

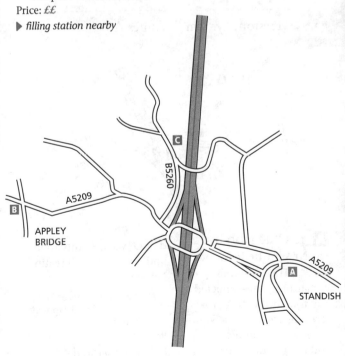

A The Hayrick
Leyland
© (01772) 434668
A modern eating house
with restaurant, bar and
family lounge open every
day. The entrance is
difficult to find.

Open noon– 9.30pm
Sunday–Thursday;
noon–10pm Friday and
Saturday
Price: ££

29 Preston, Lytham St Annes A6

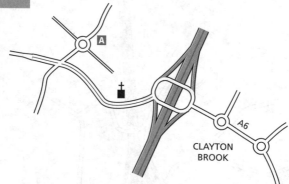

A Ye Olde Hob Inn
Nr Whittle-le-Woods
© (01772) 36863
A charming half-timbered
and thatched cottage row
forming a low-beamed pub
with saloon, lounge bars
and restaurant open seven

days a week. Family room
and outside bench seating.
No dogs.

Last orders for meals at 2pm
and 9pm. Closed Monday
evenings
Price: ££
▶ *filling station nearby*

31 Preston A59

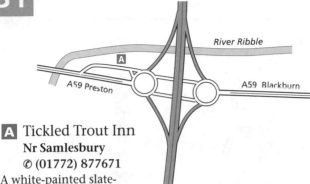

River Ribble

A59 Preston

A59 Blackburn

A Tickled Trout Inn
Nr Samlesbury
© (01772) 877671

A white-painted slate-roofed hotel on the southern bank of the River Ribble visible from the junction. The original building contains a comfortable restaurant and roomy bar with lounge service. Adjacent is a modern 72-bedroom extension with conference facilities and a small leisure complex. Dogs permitted for residents only.

Last orders for meals 2pm and 9.45pm
Price: £££; set lunch at £18
▶ *filling station adjacent*

Garstang A6 32

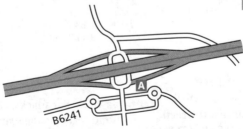

B6241

A Taverne Fayre
Broughton
© (01772) 866066

Opened in 1994, this is a large roadhouse with all the expected facilities for meals and children's entertainment. Dogs prohibited.

Last orders for weekday meals at 2pm and 10pm. Open all day Sundays from noon to 10pm
Price: ££

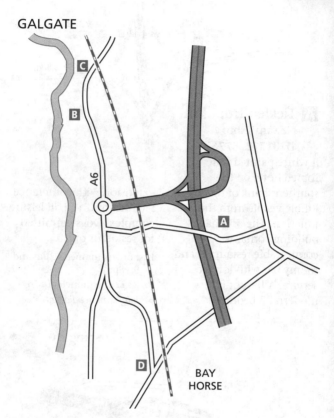

GALGATE

A6

BAY
HORSE

A Hampson
House Hotel
Hampson Green
© (01524) 751158

An attractive converted farmhouse with some modern extensions, a large garden and surrounded by meadows. Lunches and dinners in a fully licensed restaurant open seven days a week; bar snacks, coffee and tea. Outside seating and playground. No dogs off leads. Coaches by arrangement.

Daily meals from 12 to 2pm
and 7 to 9.30pm
Sunday lunches extended to
3.30pm
Price: £££ in restaurant

B Canalside Craft Centre
Galgate
☎ (01524) 752223

Stone-built farm buildings with rough-cast additions by the canal. Buffet-style restaurant lunches only, with outside seating on the canal bank and facilities for the disabled. Children's playground and dogs permitted. Clean and friendly.

Last orders for meals 5.30pm; closed Mondays except bank holidys
Price: £

C Plough Inn
Galgate
☎ (01524) 751337

White pebbledashed pub on a busy road serving bar meals and snacks at lunchtime only.

Lunch served noon–2pm
Price: £
▶ *filling station nearby*

D Bay Horse Inn
Bay Horse
☎ (01524) 791204

Some distance from the junction, this is a quiet and attractive 17th-century pub on the edge of a secluded village. Bar snacks, lunches and evening meals seven days a week. Garden and car park behind.

Last orders for meals 2pm and 9pm; open from noon to 9pm Sundays
Price: ££–££

Lancaster, Kirkby Lonsdale, Morecambe, Heysham A683 **34**

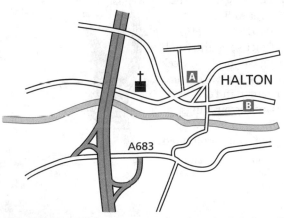

M6

A The White Lion
Halton
✆ (01524) 811210

A pleasant white-painted country inn opposite a mediæval gatehouse. It provides bar lunches and evening meals. Beer garden. Children allowed but no dogs.

Evening meals until 8.30pm (9pm Friday and Saturday); closed for food Sunday evenings

Price: £

B The Greyhound
Halton
✆ (01524) 811356

A stone building with some modern extensions. Lunches and evening meals all week. Some outside seating and children's play area. Dogs allowed (as well they should be at a pub called the Greyhound).

Meals daily 12–2pm and 6–8pm but closed Sunday evenings

Price: ££

▶ *Note: these two listings are only reached by a narrow twisting lane and a bridge 1m83 (6ft) in width. Not suitable for large cars or caravans.*

---

35 Carnforth, Morecambe A601(M)

A The Eagle's Head
Over Kellet
✆ (01524) 732457

An attractive country pub serving bar meals all week including Sunday evenings. Beer garden in very pleasant surroundings. Family room for children. Dogs prohibited.

Meals daily 12–2pm and 7–9pm
Price: ££

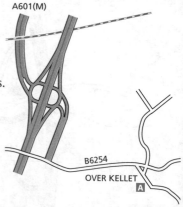

36 South Lakes, Kendal, Barrow A590
Kirkby Lonsdale, Skipton A65

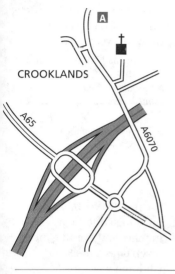

A Crooklands Hotel
Crooklands
© (015395) 67432

Formerly a country inn lying by the Lancaster Canal. Extensive alterations and additions now provide accommodation in an annexe. Coffee shop, bars, restaurant and a carvery provide meals seven days a week.

Meals daily from noon to 2pm and 7 to 9pm
Price: £–£££

Kendal, Sedbergh A684 **37**

▶ *Not a house to be seen either side of the motorway. A suitable area for picnics, but mainly on the asphalt lay-bys provided, since getting further off the road is difficult.*

Brough A685 Appleby B6260 **38**

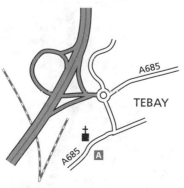

A Cross Keys
Nr Tebay
© (015396) 24240

An attractive 400-year-old family-run village coaching inn with accommodation. Hot and cold home-cooked bar food all week and a beer garden with children's area. Dogs confined to the car park. Coaches and caravans welcomed.

Daily meals 12–2.30pm and 6–9pm
▶ *specialities: steak and mushroom pies*
Price: £
▶ *filling station on the way*

A The Greyhound Hotel
Shap
© (01931) 716474

An attractive coaching inn dating from 1680 with the original old bedrooms at the rear. Serves breakfast, morning coffee, bar lunches and evening meals seven days a week. Children welcomed.

Weekday meals from 12–2pm and 6.45–8.45pm
Sunday meals from 12–2pm and 7–8.45pm
Price: £
▶ *filling station on the approach road*

    ▶ *An ideal picnic area offering wide views of open countryside and distant hills. Unlimited opportunities to pull off the road.*

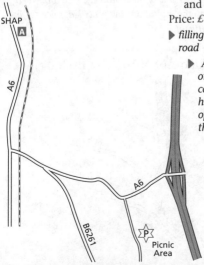

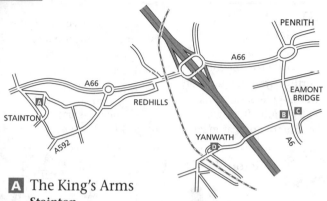

A The King's Arms
Stainton
℡ (01768) 862778

A village pub of character dating from 1721. Serves bar meals all week including Sunday evening. Beer garden, patio and family room. Only guide dogs allowed inside.

Meals daily 12–1.45pm and 6.30–9pm (Sunday evening 7–9pm)

Price: £

B Crown Hotel
Eamont Bridge
℡ (01768) 892092

A coaching inn dating from the 18th-century on the old A6. Now offering bed and breakfast, with restaurant and bar meals available seven days a week. Children's room and beer garden. Well-behaved dogs allowed.

Daily midday meals 12–3pm
Weekday evenings 5.30–10pm
Sunday evenings 7–9.30pm
▶ *specialities: home-made steak and kidney pie*
Price: £

C Beehive Inn
Eamont Bridge
℡ (01768) 862081

An old pub dated 1727 facing the Crown Hotel. Serving coffee, grills and bar snacks all week including Sunday evening. Beer garden and children's playground. Dogs permitted.

Daily meals 12–2.30pm and 6–9pm; Sundays open from noon to 10.30pm
▶ *specialities: Cumberland sausage*
Price: £
▶ *filling station close by*

D The Yanwath
Gate Inn
Yanwath
✆ (01768) 862386
Further from the junction ,
this is a pleasant small
village pub offering a
restaurant and bar meals

seven days a week. Outside
seating and informal car
parking. Dogs are tolerated,
children welcomed.

Daily meals 12–2.30pm and
6.30–9.30pm (Sunday
evenings 7–9pm)
Price: ££

41 Wigton B5305

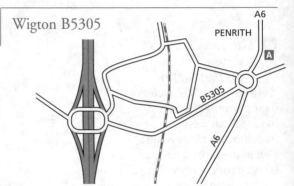

A Stoneybeck Inn
Penrith
✆ (01768) 862369
On the old A6 main
crossroads with the B5305,
and once, no doubt, a
coaching inn. Bar meals
and restaurant open all

week Large car park with
caravan site adjacent.
Children allowed in family
room. No dogs inside.

Weekday meals 11am–2.30pm
and 6–9pm; Sunday
12–2.30pm and 6–9pm
Price: £££

42 Carlisle, Penrith A6

A The Green Bank
Carleton
✆ (01228) 28846
A semi-urban pub in a
lightly built-up area
providing bar meals except

Wednesday evenings. No
dogs.

Daily meals 12–2pm and
6–8.30 (Sunday evenings
7–9pm)
Price: £
▶ *filling station close by*

B Carrow House Hotel
© (01228) 32073

A modern hotel on the junction roundabout, offering bar food all week as well as full restaurant and hotel services. Children welcomed, but no dogs.

Meals daily 12–2.15pm and 5.30 to 9.15pm (Sunday lunch extended to 3pm)

Price: ££

▶ filling station nearby

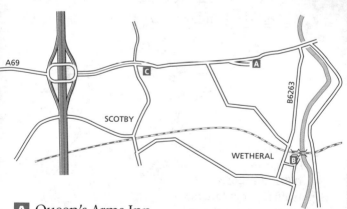

A Queen's Arms Inn
Warwick on Eden
© (01228) 560699

A fine old black and white coaching inn with bar meals available daily. Children's playground.

Dogs outside only.

Meals weekdays 12–2pm and 6–9pm; Sunday 12–2pm and 7–9pm

▶ specialities: home-made steak pie

Price: £–££

B Crown Hotel
Wetheral
✆ (01228) 561888

A large Georgian country coaching inn and hotel. Comfortable bars and restaurant. Behind the frontage there is a large car park and extensive new buildings for conferences and business purposes. Dogs permitted. Children's playground and family room.

Meals daily 12–2pm and 7–9.30pm (last orders Sunday evening at 9pm)

▶ specialities: Cumbrian cheeses
Price: £££ in restaurant; £ in bar

C The Waterloo
Aglionby
✆ (01228) 513347

A small wayside pub offering bar meals all week including Sunday evening. Outside seating and children welcomed. No dogs.

Meals daily 12–2pm and 6.30–8.45pm; closed Mondays
Price: £–£££

44 Carlisle, Longtown A7

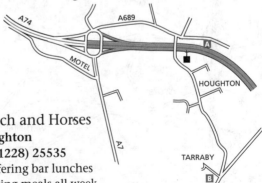

A Coach and Horses
Houghton
✆ (01228) 25535

A pub offering bar lunches and evening meals all week except Sunday evenings.
Price: £–££

B The Near Boot
Tarraby
✆ (01228) 29547

A country pub serving bar lunches only, all week. Beer garden and outside seating.

Lunches from noon to 2pm; closed Monday
Price: £

Junctions **1** to **9**

This motorway connects Manchester with the M6 going north, and passes through some pleasant scenery with fine views of the Pennine Hills.

Atherton, Leigh A6 **4**

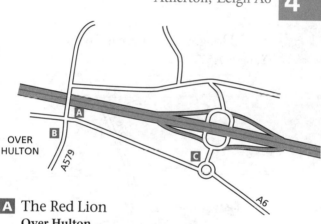

A The Red Lion
Over Hulton
℡ (01204) 63257

An old stone-built coaching inn refurbished in 1905, with an 18th-century cottage annexe. Lounge bar, restaurant and family room. Friendly atmosphere and good appearance. No dogs.

Last orders for weekday meals at 2pm and 10pm. Open Sundays from noon to 10pm

Price: £££

filling station nearby

B The Hulton Arms
Over Hulton
℡ (01204) 61010

A traditional black and white public house on a crossroads. Hot and cold food, lunches and early evening meals, except Sunday nights. No dogs.

Last orders for meals at 2pm and 8pm. Open from midday to 6pm Sundays

Price: ££

▶ *filling station nearby*

C Watergate Toll
Over Hulton
© (01204) 64989

A modernized toll-house in sight of the motorway. *À la carte* menu, hot and cold bar meals all day, every day. Some outside seating and a family room. No dogs.

Open daily from 11.30am to 9pm (later on Friday & Saturday) and noon to 9pm Sunday

Price: £££

▶ *filling station on the road from the junction*

---

5 West Houghton, St Helens A676, Wigan A577

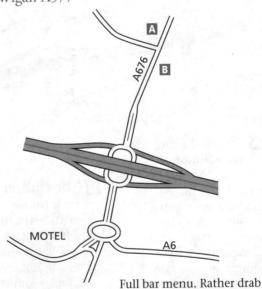

A The Three Pigeons
Hunger Hill
© (01204) 61678

A stone-built modernized pub on a busy main road with a small beer garden.

Full bar menu. Rather drab surroundings. No dogs.

Last orders for meals 3pm and 11pm (10.30pm Sundays). Open from noon to 11pm Fridays

Price: ££

▶ *filling station nearby*

B The Tavern and Farmhouse Restaurant
Hunger Hill
(01204) 656638

Based on a stone farmhouse and brick outhouse with extensive additions. The restaurant serves business lunches and dinners. The interior of the Tavern seems designed to please the youthful; bar meals and early evening meals on offer. Children are welcomed and there is some outside seating. Numerous arcade games and piped music. No dogs indoors.

Last orders for meals 2pm and 10pm. No Saturday lunches

Price: £££

▶ *filling station on the road from the junction*

Chorley, Horwich A6027 **6**

A The Royal Oak
Horwich
(01254) 201445

A small cream-painted country pub on a main road overlooking fields. Home-cooked lunches and suppers all week. Outside seating and a patio. Dogs allowed.

Last orders for meals at 2pm and 9pm every day

Price: ££

▶ *filling station on the road from the junction*

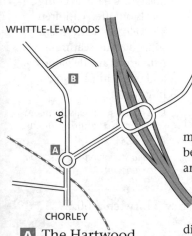

WHITTLE-LE-WOODS

CHORLEY

A The Hartwood
Chorley
© (01257) 269966

A late Georgian mansion converted, with modern additions, into a 10-room hotel and pub restaurant serving lunches and dinners to non-residents. The rear gardens have been bulldozed away to enlarge the car parking. Dogs permitted and children catered for.

Open daily from midday; bar meals till 10pm, restaurant until 10.50pm

Price: ££

B The Sea View
Whittle-le-Woods
© (01257) 270262

A traditional old pub; home-made food available for lunch and evening meals. Proud of its draught beers. Some outside seating and on a busy road but with views of the countryside behind and, on a clear day, a distant view (30kms) of the sea. Children's play area; dogs allowed.

Last orders for meals at 2pm and 9pm (8.30pm on Sunday)

Price: ££

▶ filling station on the road from the junction

C The Red Cat
© (01257) 263966

An attractive old stone-built country pub, now painted black and white, on a busy road. Bar, restaurant, pizzeria, children's playground and outside seating. It is necessary to drive past the premises and turn first left to gain access. No dogs.

Last orders for meals at 2pm and 10pm

Price: £££

Junctions **1** to **38**

including A627(M)

Like the M5, this major motorway ignores the influence of London, linking Liverpool on the west coast to Hull on the east. In doing so it traverses a range of environments from urban haze to the high open spaces of the Pennines.

Huyton A5080 **5**

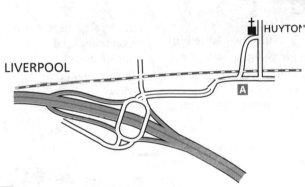

A Derby Lodge Hotel
Huyton
℡ (0151) 480 4440

A merchant's red sandstone mansion converted into a hotel demanding a smart standard of dress at all times. Restaurant and patio bar. An attractive garden is overlooked by a housing estate. Adjoining stables have been converted into a Wine Bar called Natterjacks. No facilities for children or dogs.

Last orders for meals at 2.30pm and 9.30pm

Price: £££

▶ *filling station on the road from the junction*

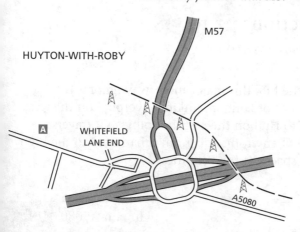

M57

HUYTON-WITH-ROBY

A

WHITEFIELD
LANE END

A5080

A The Hare & Hounds
Whitefield Lane End

A brick and timbered 1920s building serving hot and cold bar food at midday and evenings. Beer garden and large car park at rear. Good traditional atmosphere.

Last orders 2pm and 9.30pm
Price: ££
▶ *filling station nearby*

7 Widnes A569

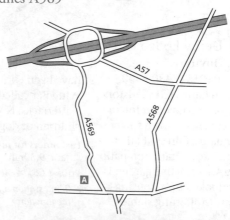

A57

A568

A569

A

A Black Horse Hotel
Widnes
© (0151) 424 3729

Victorian brick and stone building modernized as a trendy pub with bar and restaurant and an adjoining bar in the old stable block.

Last orders for meals at 2.30pm and 9pm

Price: ££

▶ *filling station opposite*

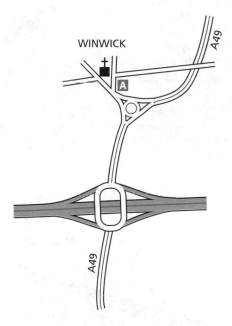

A The Swan
Winwick
© (01925) 631416

A brick and timber building; offers hot and cold home-cooked bar food. Some outside tables and children's playground. Dogs permitted.

Last orders for meals at 2.30pm and 9.30pm

Price: £££

▶ *filling station nearby*

M62

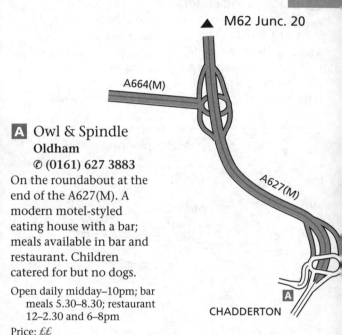

▲ M62 Junc. 20

A664(M)

A627(M)

A Owl & Spindle
Oldham
✆ (0161) 627 3883
On the roundabout at the
end of the A627(M). A
modern motel-styled
eating house with a bar;
meals available in bar and
restaurant. Children
catered for but no dogs.

Open daily midday–10pm; bar
meals 5.30–8.30; restaurant
12–2.30 and 6–8pm
Price: ££

A

CHADDERTON

21 Milnrow, Shaw A663

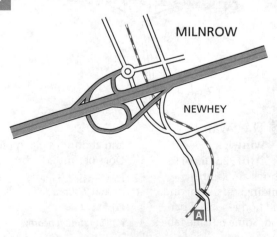

MILNROW

NEWHEY

A

A Ladybarn Hotel
Elizabeth Way
Milnrow
℗ **(01706) 355402**

A stalwart stone building by the ramp over a bridge in this architecturally interesting village (note dates inscribed in the doorstones). Béing refurbished under new management so it is advisable to telephone in advance. Large car park with fields behind.

No hours or price details currently available

Denshaw A672 **22**

▶ *High up on the Pennines, this offers an ideal picnic spot. Not a house to be seen but an unending line of lamp standards along the motorway indicates the presence of man.*

Brighouse A644 Huddersfield A62 **25**

BRIGHOUSE

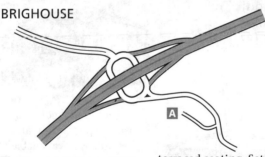

A The Old Corn Mill
Nr Brighouse
℗ **(01484) 400069**

A substatial stone-built corn mill with dependent buildings, lavishly converted into a restaurant, bistro, bars, conference and banqueting facilities, nightclub and outside terraced seating. Set in a wooded valley with children's playground and dogs allowed.

Last orders for meals at 2pm (3pm Sundays) and 10pm; closed for meals on Sunday evenings

Price: £££

▶ *filling station on the road from the junction*

Leeds, Dewsbury A653 28

A The White Bear
Topcliffe
© (0113) 253 2768

Very close to the junction, this pub offers a full range of services; morning coffee, bar and restaurant meals at midday and evenings. Children's playground; no dogs.

Open daily midday–10.30pm (11pm on Saturday); food served all day

Price: £££

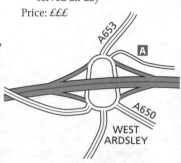

---

30 Rothwell, Wakefield A642

A Spindle Tree
Stanley
© (01924) 826353

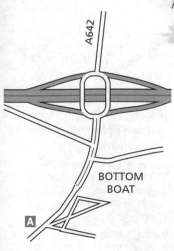

A cream- and green-painted roadside pub; bright and cheerful. Meals available at the bar, restaurant and carvery all week including Sunday evening. Outside seating and children's playground. No dogs indoors.

Last orders for meals at 2pm and 10pm; 2.15pm and 9.30pm on Sundays at the bar; closed Mondays

Price: ££–£££

32   Pontefract, Castleford A639

A   Parkside Inne
Pontefract
℡ (01977) 709911

An old brick farmhouse has been converted into a modern complex of bars, restaurant, hotel and conference centre. The long bar is extravagantly furnished and the atmosphere is lively. Extensive outside seating and lavish children's areas. No dogs.

Last orders for meals at 2pm and 10pm; (9pm on Sundays)

▶ *specialities: vast Yorkshire puddings*

Price: £–£££

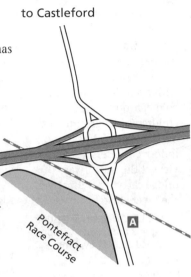

to Castleford

Pontefract Race Course

---

34   Selby, Doncaster A19

EGGBOROUGH

A19

Canal

A19

WHITLEY

A   George & Dragon
Whitley
℡ (01977) 661319

A 1930s cream-painted pub. Bar meals at lunch and evenings every day including Sunday. Children's play area, fishpond and outside seating with car park in front. No dogs.

Last orders for meals at 2pm and 9.30pm daily

Price: £

A The Ferryboat Inn
Boothferry
© (01430) 430300

A whitewashed nondescript building on the bank of the River Ouse with restaurant, hot and cold bar food. Large children's playground and outside seating but no dogs indoors. It offers a striking view of the motorway bridge carrying traffic over the River Ouse.

Last orders for meals at 2.30pm (3pm Sunday) and 9.30pm; closed Sunday evenings

Price: ££

▶ *filling station on the road from the junction.*

B The Wellington Hotel
Howden
© (01430) 430258

An old coaching inn in the centre of this interesting and historic town with its Minster and the restored Great Hall of the Prince Bishop of Durham's summer palace. Accommodation, restaurant with home-cooked bar meals and beer garden. No dogs.

Last orders for meals at 2pm and 10pm

Price: ££

C Bowmans Hotel
Howden
© (01430) 430805

Next to The Wellington, Bowmans is another old coaching inn also with accommodation, restaurant and bar lunches. Dogs permitted.

Last orders for lunches at 2pm (2.30pm Sundays); evening meals Fridays and Saturdays only, until 9pm

Price: £££

▶ *filling station on the road from the junction to Howden*

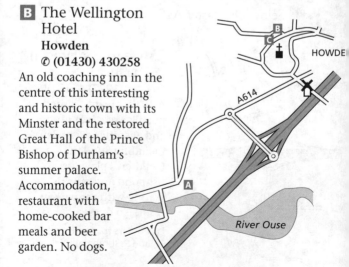

Junctions `1` to `15`

The southern part of the urban orbital system round Manchester. This is a commuter and industrial motorway with little to commend it to the travelling tourist. There are few places to break off so one would be well advised to hurry on.

Irlam, Eccles A57 `2`

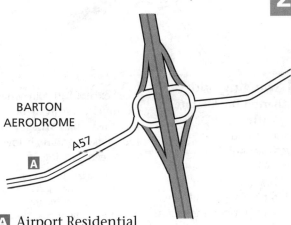

BARTON AERODROME

A57

A

A Airport Residential Hotel
Eccles
℗ (0161) 789 6543

A former farmhouse converted into a hotel with 10 bedrooms and the old farm buildings standing empty behind. On the perimeter of Barton Aerodrome grass field. Lunches served seven days a week but evening meals on Fridays and Saturdays only. Outside seating with traditional foods and ales. A southerly wind may bring evidence of the sewage treatment works on the far side of the Manchester Ship Canal. No dogs.

Last orders for meals at 2pm and 10.30pm (Friday and Saturday evenings only)

Price: £££

▶ *filling station nearby*

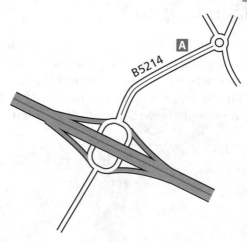

A Swinging Bridge
Barton Dock Estate
✆ (0161) 748 3388

A modernized rough-cast public house with a restaurant, bars, beer garden and children's playground. The restaurant is open for lunch and supper seven days a week except Saturday when bar lunches are available. By a busy dual carriageway roundabout and no bridge to be seen. No dogs.

Open daily from noon to 9.30pm; lunch served 12–2.30, evening meals 5.30–10.30pm
Price: £££

8 Sale A6144

A The Jacksons Boat
Sale
✆ (0161) 973 3208

An interesting old brick waterside inn by the River Mersey, lying at the end of a lane with pleasant garden and children's playground adjacent to a golf-course. Bar food only. Dogs and children allowed.

Bar meals from midday to 2pm
▶ *specialities: Sunday roast*
Price: £

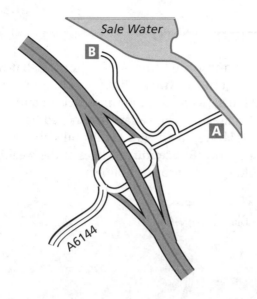

B Deckers Restaurant
Sale
© (0161) 962 0118
A modern purpose-built restaurant open seven days a week on the shore of the recreational Sale Water Park. Owned by the local authority and shares a large car park with the adjacent water sport facilities. Part of the recently created Mersey Valley Visitors' Park.

Last orders for meals at 2.30pm and 11pm (10.30 on Sunday)

Price: ££

M65 Blackburn ◀

▶Colne

Junctions 6 to 14

At present an isolated stretch of motorway that will eventually join the M61. It links the old mill towns of Blackburn, Accrington, Burnley, Nelson and Colne. An area of deep valleys overlooked by the open fells above, filled with textile mills and villages since the 18th century. Echoes of the wealth of the old cotton barons still linger.

6   Blackburn A6119

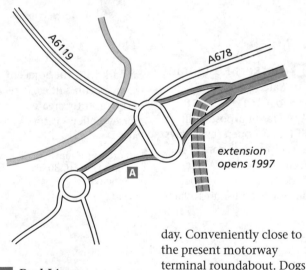

extension opens 1997

A Red Lion
Blackburn
✆ (01254) 695495
An unexciting public house serving bar lunches every day. Conveniently close to the present motorway terminal roundabout. Dogs allowed.

Last orders at 3pm on weekdays and 2.45pm on Sunday
Price: £

A Dunkenhalgh Hotel
Clayton le Moors
© (01254) 398021
A large turreted country house converted into a luxury 79-room hotel and restaurant. Family room and no dogs.

Last orders for meals in the restaurant at 2pm and 9.45pm every day

Price: *££££*

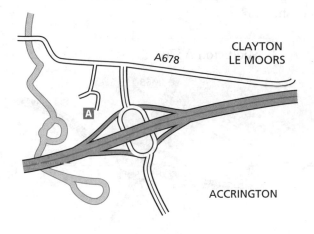

M66 Manchester ◀ ▶Rochdale

Junctions 1 to 5 & 11 to 12

At present this is a short urban motorway with a break between Junctions 5 and 11, which may finally form the eastern ringway round Manchester. It gives quick access from the northern mill towns to Manchester city centre and there are therefore few opportunities or enticements to leave it. There is some interesting landscape to the north of the M62.

5 Middleton A576

A Three Arrows
Middleton
✆ **(0161) 643 5278**

A pleasant and recently refurbished old-style country pub close by the terminal junction roundabout. On sunny days peacocks may present themselves from neighbouring ground. Dogs permitted.

Open daily from noon to 7pm and noon to 2pm on Sunday
Price: £

12   Bredbury A601

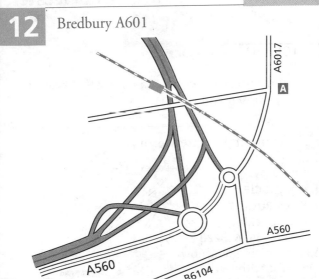

A **Horsfield Arms**
Bredbury
© (0161) 430 6390

A well-maintained modernized country pub with a full lunch menu Monday to Friday. Mainly used by local businessmen from the industrial estate nearby. No dogs, but children allowed for lunch.

Last orders for lunch (weekdays only) 2pm
Price: £
▶ *filling station on the road from the junction*

Denton ◀
▶Mottram in Longdendale

M67

Junctions **1** to **4**

A short urban motorway approaching Manchester from the east and linking with the uncompleted M66 and M63 orbital. It offers no opportunity for stopping.

Junctions 1 to 2

This short motorway cuts off a corner to Leicester between the M6 and the M1.

1 Nuneaton, Letterworth A5

HINCKLEY

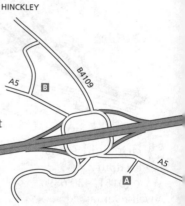

A Barnacles Restaurant
Nr Hinckley
✆ (01455) 633220

An old brick building now converted, with recent additions, into a restaurant open for lunch and dinner each weekday except Saturday evenings. A retail shop adjacent offers seafood. Pleasant green surroundings which can include grazing goats; no dogs. Worth visiting.

Last orders for weekday meals at 1.45pm and 10pm. Closed Sundays.
Price: £££
▶ *filling station on the road from the junction.*

B Hinckley Knight
Hinckley
✆ (01455) 610773

A modern attractive building with restaurants and bars open all and every day including Sunday. Comfortable and kitsch. No dogs. Children allowed any time in the restaurant and until 6.30pm in the bar.

Open daily from noon until 9.30pm and all day Sunday
Price: £££
▶ *filling station nearby*

Glasgow ◀ ▶ Carlisle **M74**

Junctions **4** to **15**

This has become a very different road since 1994 when major works commenced on the southern half of the old A74 to upgrade it to motorway status. Much of the new road has followed a parallel course so that stretches of splendid dual carriageway have been down-rated to B-road status. There will be a progression from A74 to A74(M) to M74. When complete it is intended that the M74 will be redesignated and junctions re-numbered as part of the M6 but Scots pride dies hard.

Douglas A70 **5**

▶ *From Junction 4 to Junction 11 there is nothing to stop for unless the Strathclyde Park or Chatelherault Country Park, both off Junction 5, are of interest.*

Douglas A70 **12**

A Cairn Lodge Services
© (01555) 851177

This is the exception that proves the rule; an official motorway service station imaginatively developed around one of Castle Douglas's gate houses and run as a family concern which it is a pleasure to visit. Complete service station facilities are provided and conditions including the disabled. A craft shop and visitors' centre are featured and home cooking is on offer.

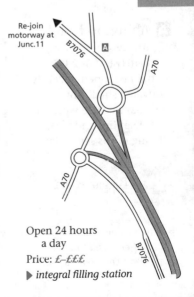

Re-join motorway at Junc.11

Open 24 hours a day
Price: £–£££
▶ *integral filling station*

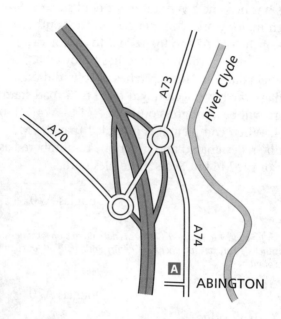

A70

A73

River Clyde

A74

A

ABINGTON

A Abington Hotel
Abington
© **(01864) 502467**
An old-fashioned, recently renovated small hotel in the village centre with full hotel facilities and a bar, offering meals seven days a week. Several touring club recommendations.

Open for meals from midday. Last orders for lunch 3pm; supper 9pm
▶ *specialities: steak and kidney pie*
Price: ££

14 Biggar A702

▶ *In the nearby village of Crawford there are two adjoining hotels, the Tudor House and Crawford House offering bar meals at midday and in the evenings, but this is not an appealing village.*

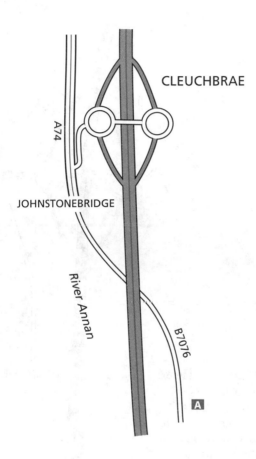

A Dinwoodie Lodge Hotel
✆ **(01576) 470289**
A listed Grade B whinstone building visible from the motorway when travelling north, converted into a hotel with restaurant and lounge bar. Children are welcome and dogs allowed. Facilities for the disabled.

Last orders for meals at 2.30pm and 8.45pm daily
Price: ££

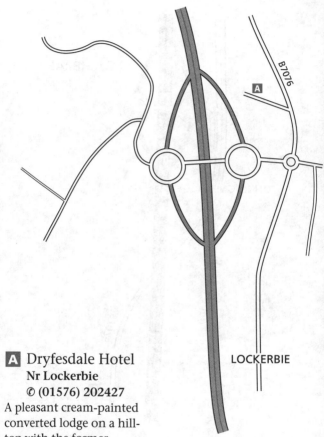

LOCKERBIE

A Dryfesdale Hotel
Nr Lockerbie
© (01576) 202427
A pleasant cream-painted converted lodge on a hilltop with the former steading and other buildings forming annexes, with 15 bedrooms. It has much to commend it for a leisurely break. Restaurant and bar meals served in a well-kept garden, weather permitting. No specific facilities for children due to the extensive gardens and dogs are permitted.

Last orders for meals at 2pm and 9pm every day
Price: *££–£££*

18 Lockerbie B723 Dumfries (A709)
restricted access, exit northbound, entry southbound

LOCKERBIE

A Queens Hotel
Nr Lockerbie
✆ (01576) 202415

A large redstone country house and garden with a modern 21-bed extension, conference centre and leisure complex. With restaurant, cocktail and lounge bar serving bar meals. Children welcome and dogs allowed. Garden extends to 3 acres.

Meals all day until 9.30pm
Price: ££

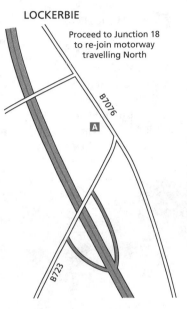

Proceed to Junction 18 to re-join motorway travelling North

Eaglesfield B722 20

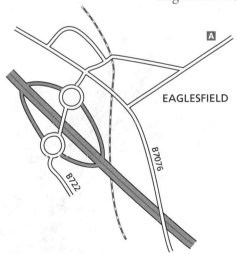

A The Courtyard
Eaglesfield
© (01461) 500215
A stone-built private village house now offering bed and breakfast, with a restaurant and small bar. Children's playground and car parking at the rear, with some outside seating. The restaurant holds a children's licence.

Last orders for meals at 2pm and 9pm; closed for meals on Mondays
▶ *speciality: pork fillet*
Price: ££

21 *restricted access; split junction*

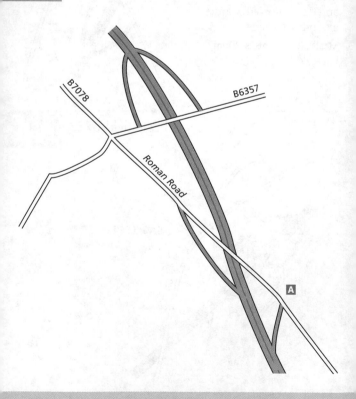

A The Mill Barn
Restaurant
Grahamshill
© **(01461) 800344**
A group of stone-built farm
buildings now operating as
a restaurant on first-floor
level, under an open
trussed roof. Serves bar
meals at all times including
Sunday evenings. Chalet
accommodation also
available.

Open daily 11am–10pm; food
  available all day
Price: ££

Longton A6071 Gretna Green B6076 **24**
restricted access

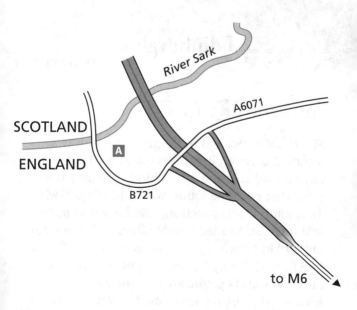

A The Gretna
Chase Hotel
Gretna Green
✆ (01461) 337517

The first or last hotel in England, depending upon your direction of travel. A late Georgian private house forming a comfortable hotel with a spectacularly colourful garden on the bank of the River Sark. Outside seating. Meals available all week including Sunday evenings in the restaurant or lounge bar. Ideal for runaway wedding receptions.

Last orders for meals at 3pm and 10pm

Price: *££*

Scotland
M8   Edinburgh ◀

▶Glasgow

Junctions **1** to **31**

Still to be completed or upgraded to motorway standard between Junctions 6 and 8. This is a boring road and best left behind. The only stopping place that could be found was at Junction 6 where, 1km south of the junction, there is a new motel and restaurant called The Newhouse. The surrounding terrain between Junctions 6 and 30 is all urban. Junction 31 finally leaves Glasgow behind and offers an untidy picnic area on the bank of the River Clyde looking across at Dunbarton Castle.

Bonnybridge ◀
▶Kinkardine Bridge

Junctions **1** to **3**

A short motorway connecting the M9 and M80, and ending near Kincardine Bridge.

Denny, Falkirk A883 **1**

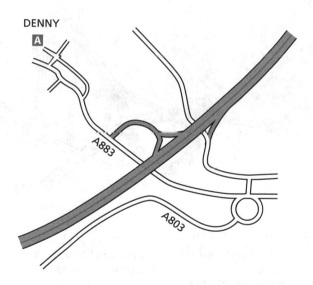

A The Horsemill Inn
✆ **(01324) 822241**
A small converted farmhouse and steading serving lunches, suppers and high teas all week including Sunday evenings. Children's playground.

Lunch daily 12–2.15pm; evening meals 6–9pm
High teas Saturday and Sunday 5–10pm
Price: ££

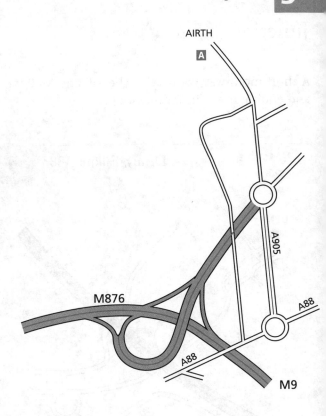

A Airth Castle Hotel & Country Club
Airth
℗ (01324) 831411

A mediæval castle (dating back to the early 14th century), originally home to the Barons of Airth and Lords of Elphinstone converted into a 4-star hotel. Large gardens and park, sports centre and swimming pool. Convenient for those visiting the 'Pineapple' at Dunmore Park nearby. No dogs indoors; children welcomed. Extensive landscaped gardens.

Lunch daily 12.30–1.45pm; evening meals 7–9.45 pm
▶ *specialities: local Scots produce*
Price: £££
▶ *filling station nearby*

Edinburgh ◀ ▶Stirling   M9

Junctions **1** to **11**

Starting near Edinburgh Airport, this motorway passes some old slag heaps and workings before going by the impressive ruins of Linlithgow Palace and the historic site of Bannockburn. It ends under the walls of Stirling Castle.

Junction 2 is a *restricted access* junction, exit eastbound, entry westbound. It is useful to those exiting at Junction 3 (*see* below) and wishing to rejoin the motorway going west.

---

3 Linlithgow, Bo'ness A904
restricted access; exit westbound, entry eastbound.

A **Earl o'Moray Inn**
Linlithgow
☎ (01506) 842229

Lying on a minor road connecting Linlithgow and Bonsyde. A country house converted to an 8-bedroom hotel with fine views to the south. Morning coffee, full afternoon teas, lunches and dinners daily. Children welcomed; no dogs indoors. Garden and grounds extend to six acres.

Lunch served 12–2.30pm; evening meals 5–9.30pm
Sunday lunch 12.30–2.30pm
Price: *££££*; set menu £30 by an award-winning chef; *££* bar snacks available

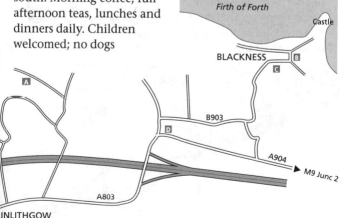

▶ *LINLITHGOW has many restaurants, bars and hotels, as would be expected in this historic city with its ruined royal palace.*

B The Hamlet
Blackness
℗ (01506) 834251

An old-fashioned tearoom with gift shop. Fully licensed, serving bistro lunches, teas and evening meals seven days a week.

Meals daily 11am–8pm; booking recommended after 6pm
Price: ££

C The Blackness Inn
Blackness
℗ (01506) 834252

A typical public house with full bar facilities, midday and evening meals. Bed and breakfast available at competitive rates.

Lunch daily 12–2pm; evening meals 6–10pm
▶ *specialities: seafood*
Price: £–££

▶ *BLACKNESS (taking the A803 north at the junction and re-joining the M9 back at Junction 2 to go westwards.)*

D Champany Inn
Champany
℗ (01506) 834532

Lying on the B903 to Blackness. A country inn of extremely high quality and winners of various gastronomic awards. Not for those in a hurry or trying to save money.

Lunch daily 12–2pm; evening meals 6.30–10pm. Restaurant closed Sunday
▶ *specialities: Aberdeen Angus steaks and Shetland salmon*
Price: £££ (bar); ££££ (restaurant)

5 Bo'ness B904 (A904)

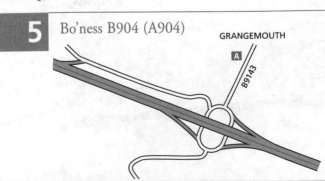

A Inchyra Grange Hotel

Grangemouth
℗ **(01324) 711911**

A large Victorian country house converted into a 3-star hotel with leisure centre and sports club. Restaurant and bar serving meals to casual visitors.

Lunch 12–2pm, Sundays 12.30–2pm; evening meals 7–9.30pm

Price: £££

A Airth Castle Hotel & Country Club

Airth
℗ **(01324) 831411**

A mediæval castle (dating back to the early 14th century), originally home to the Barons of Airth and Lords of Elphinstone, now converted into a 4-star hotel. Large gardens and park, sports centre and swimming pool. Convenient for those visiting the 'Pineapple' at Dunmore Park nearby. No dogs indoors; children welcomed. Extensive landscaped gardens.

Lunch daily 12.30–1.45pm; evening meals 7–9.45 pm
▶ *specialities: local Scots produce*
Price: £££
▶ *filling station nearby*

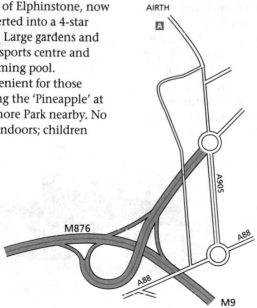

M9

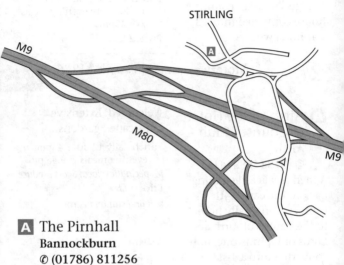

STIRLING

M9

M80

M9

A The Pirnhall
Bannockburn
© (01786) 811256

A converted old building with modern extensions to the rear. Food and drink all day seven days a week. Children's adventure playground and facilities for the disabled.

Morning coffee from 10am
Meals served daily from
  11.30am to 10pm; Sundays
  noon to 10pm
Price: £-££

Edinburgh ◀   ▶Perth   M90

Junctions **1** to **11**

The only Scottish motorway that could be described as scenic and that gives promise of the Highlands beyond. The approach road from the South crosses the Firth of Forth by the superb suspension bridge a mile or so upstream of the venerable and even-more-superb cantilever rail bridge famous throughout the world.

Inverkeithing A921   **1**

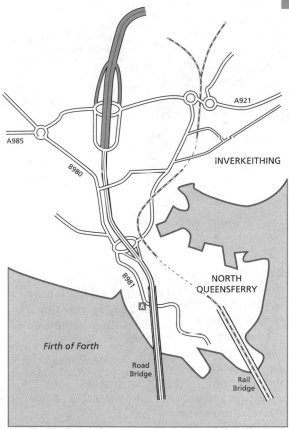

M90

A Queensferry
Lodge Hotel
North Queensferry
© (01383) 410000

A modern hotel and restaurant overlooking the Firth of Forth and the road bridge. Lounge bar with bar snacks and coffee shop. The Outside Inn Restaurant (which is inside) provides bar meals. There is also a tourist information centre and craft shop. A suitable overnight stop for the airport. A slip road at the north end of the bridge makes access easy travelling north; coming south, exit at Junction 1 for Rosyth and take the B980 off the first roundabout for North Queensferry. Although the hotel is further than usual from a junction, the spectacular view makes the detour worthwhile.

Lunch daily 12–2.30pm; evening meals 5–10pm, Sundays 4.30–10pm
Price: ££–£££

4 Kelty B914

A The Butterchurn
Kelty
© (01383) 830169

Visible on the hillside above the junction; a converted farm steading with licensed restaurant. Tea, coffee and home-cooked meals served all day. High teas at weekends. Well-suited for children and enjoys some fine views. Dogs permitted on leads.

Lunch daily 10am–5.30pm; high teas Fri, Sat and Sun 4.30–6pm
Open March–Dec 24 only
Price: ££

5 Crook of Devon B9097

A Nivingston
Country Hotel
© (01577) 850216

Lying three miles from the junction on the B9097. A large Victorian country house with extensive gardens and views of the open countryside. Midday and evening meals served seven days a week. Probably wise to book ahead. Children welcomed and dogs allowed.

Lunch daily 12–2pm; evening meals 7–9pm

Price: £££; set menu lunch £15.50, dinner £25

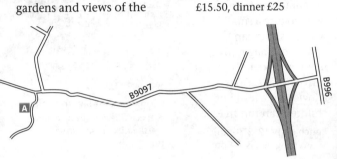

Kinross A977 6

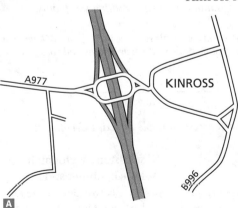

▶ This historic town is mainly known for the imprisonment of Mary Queen of Scots in Loch Leven Castle. It has many excellent hotels on the High Street and its continuation, The Muirs, such as Greens Hotel, Kirklands Hotel and The Muirs Inn.

A ## The Grouse & Claret
Heatheryford
℡ (01577) 864212

Reached by private road from the west of Junction 6. A licensed country restaurant with a garden overlooking a small loch where fishing can be arranged. Imaginative menu and friendly surroundings. Dogs allowed on a lead but children can run free.

Lunch daily 12–2.30pm;
evening meals 7–9pm

Closed on Sundays in winter
▶ *specialities: venison, salmon, fish and cheese soufflés*
Price: ££

Milnathort A91 **7**

restricted access; suitable for exit travelling south only

▶ *The Jolly Beggars and the Thistle Hotel lie in the centre of Milnathort but re-entry to the motorway is extremely lengthy and not recommended.*

---

8 Auchtermuchty A91

restricted access, suitable for exit travelling north only

A Glenfarg Hotel
Glenfarg
℡ (01577) 830665

Lying on the left of the B996 (north of the junction), this is a large traditional granite and sandstone Victorian hotel. Lunch, dinner and high tea. Beer garden at the rear.

Last orders for meals at 2pm and 9.30pm
Price: £
▶ *adjoins Glenfarg Riverside Gardens*

9 Bridge of Earn A912

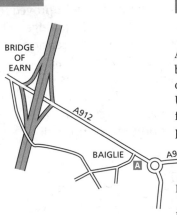

A Baiglie Inn
Abernethy
☏ **(01738) 850332**
A small country inn with
bar meals and a restaurant
open seven days a week.
Under new management
from June 1995. Dogs
permitted in the bar.

Last orders for meals at 1.45pm
and 8.45pm
Price: ££

Perth A93 11

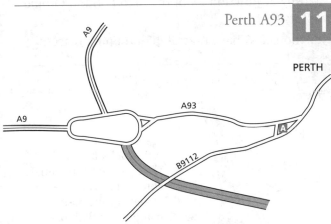

A Cherrybank Inn
Perth
☏ **(01738) 624349**
Awkwardly set below road
level and requiring a sharp
right-hand turn to get
down to the car park.
Popular with local
businessmen, it offers bar
lunches and suppers.
Adjoins Cherrybank
Gardens, open to the
public May–September.

Lunch daily 12–2pm; evening
meals 7–9pm
Price: £
▶ *filling station adjoins.*
▶ *There are many other eating
places in central Perth*

The old Great North Road is being slowly improved to motorway status along its length and, to judge from the junction numbers, there is the intention that it will finally be upgraded as far north as Newcastle if not Edinburgh. At present, it is dual carriageway all the way to Morpeth. Much of the traffic it used to carry has moved west to the M1, leaving excellent driving conditions in normal circumstances.

Southern Section
Junctions 1 to 10

Starting at Junction 23 of the M25 London Orbital motorway.

Junctions 2–5 have no suitable stopping places.

6 Welwyn Garden City A1000

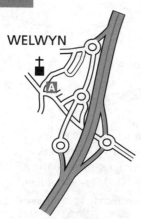

WELWYN

A fine brick-built old Georgian coaching inn. It concentrates on catering, largely for the business community, with bar lunches available in the week only. Dogs prohibited; no facilities for children.

Lunch served Mon–Fri only; last orders at 2.30pm.
▶ *specialities: fresh crab and salmon*
Price: £££
▶ *filling station nearby*

A The White Hart
Welwyn
✆ (0143871) 5353

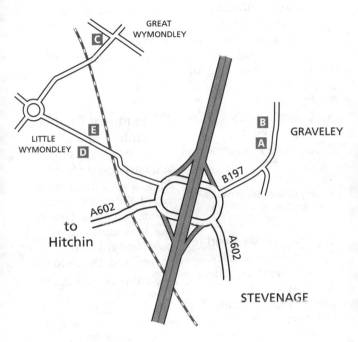

A George & Dragon
Graveley
✆ **(01438) 351362**

An old Georgian village pub on the old main road. Hot and cold bar meals; beer garden and playground. No dogs.

Last orders for meals at 2pm and 9.30pm; no evening meals on Sundays

Price: ££–£££

▶ *filling station on the road from the junction at Sainsbury's supermarket*

B The Wagon & Horses
Graveley
✆ **(01438) 367658**

Next to the George & Dragon and offering similar facilities, with the beer garden behind. No dogs allowed.

Open daily from midday until 8.30; food served all day except Sunday evenings

Price: ££

Hitchin, Stevenage (N) A602 **8**
continued

C The Green Man
Great Wymondley
℡ (01438) 357217

A brick and slated house on a village crossroads. Fresh food daily with evening bar meals. Outside seating in a neat garden with playground. Family room and dogs allowed.

Last orders for meals at 2.30pm and 9.30pm

Price: £

▶ *filling station on the road from the junction*

D The Buck's Head
Little Wymondley
℡ (01438) 353320

A white-painted pebbledashed building. Luncheons, dinners and bar snacks. *Pétanque* in the garden with a playground. Family room and dogs allowed.

Last orders for meals at 2.15pm and 9.30pm

Price: ££

E Plume of Feathers
Little Wymondley
℡ (01438) 729503

A small Georgian building. Meals served either at the bar or dining area, except Sunday evenings. Limited outside seating, family room and children's playground. Dogs allowed.

Last orders for meals at 2pm and 9pm

Price: ££

▶ *filling stations on the road from the junction*

9 Baldock, Letchworth A6141

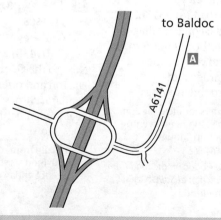

A George IV
Baldock
© (01462) 892367

A cream-painted and pebbledashed country pub on the A6141. Coffee and home-cooked food at the bar. Pleasant appearance with a well maintained and shaded beer garden with playground. No dogs.

Last orders for meals at 2pm and 9pm

Price: £££

▶ *filling station on the road from the junction.*

▶ *there are other good pubs and restaurants in Baldock*

Stotfold, Shefford A507 **10**

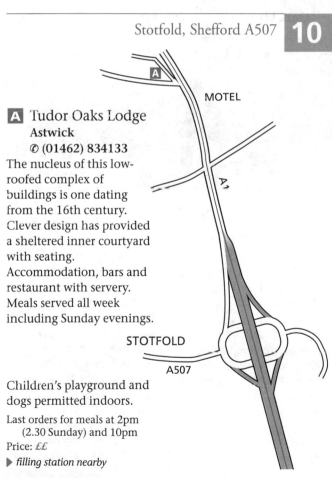

MOTEL

A Tudor Oaks Lodge
Astwick
© (01462) 834133

The nucleus of this low-roofed complex of buildings is one dating from the 16th century. Clever design has provided a sheltered inner courtyard with seating. Accommodation, bars and restaurant with servery. Meals served all week including Sunday evenings.

STOTFOLD

A507

Children's playground and dogs permitted indoors.

Last orders for meals at 2pm (2.30 Sunday) and 10pm

Price: ££

▶ *filling station nearby*

A1(M)

Middle Section
Junctions `34` to `38`

Junction 34: Blyth has several good coaching inns and pubs such as the Angel Inn and White Swan in this attractive town. Nothing was found between Junctions 35 and 38.

Northern Section
Junctions `56` to `61`

`56` Scotch Corner roundabout

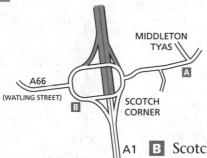

A The Shoulder of Mutton
Middle Tyas
✆ (01325) 377271

A charming old pub in a picturesque village. Hot and cold food at the bar. Restaurant meals all week days and evenings. An extensive menu (known to include wild boar); well worth a visit. No dogs.

Last orders for meals 2pm (1.30 Sunday) and 10pm
Price: ££

B Scotch Corner Hotel
✆ (01748) 850900

Famous since the early days of motoring and long before the motorways were built, this hotel used to be slightly disappointing. However, extensive work is in hand including the addition of a leisure centre, and the restaurant and bars still offer comfort.

Last orders for meals at 2pm and 10pm every day.
Price: ££–£££

57 Darlington A66(M)
restricted access

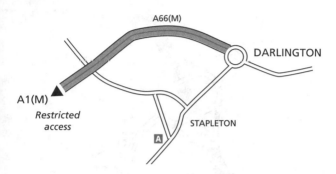

A The Bridge Inn
Stapleton
℡ (01325) 350106

A stone and half-timbered pub opposite the village green. Hot and cold food, beer garden and children welcome. Conveniently reached from the A66(M) going north only and rejoining the motorway is difficult. No dogs.

Last orders for weekday meals 2.30pm and 10pm; Sunday meals 2pm and 9.30pm

Price: £

▶ *filling station on the road from the junction*

59 Darlington, Newton Aycliffe A167

A Forester's Arms
Coatham Mundyville
℡ (01325) 320565

An attractive white-painted stone pub in pleasant surroundings. Bar meals and a simple restaurant except Sunday evenings. Outside seating and play area, but no dogs.

Last orders for weekday meals 3pm and 11pm; Sunday meals 2pm

Price: £

DARLINGTON

B Hall Garth Hotel
Brafferton
© (01325) 300400

Based on a fine 18th-century building which has been greatly extended with detached annexes to form a country club/hotel complex. Restaurant and bar. Large gardens with golf course attached.

Playground and family room but no dogs indoors.

Old Stables Bar open from 10am to 10pm every day

Restaurant last orders at 2pm and 10pm; closed Sun eves

Price: ££–£££

▶ *filling station on the road from the junction*

60 Bishop Auckland, Hartlepool, Teeside A689

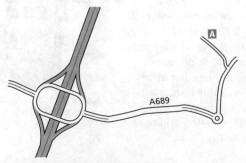

A Hardwick Hall
Hotel
Sedgefield
℗ (01740) 620253

A grey pebbledashed large country mansion standing in substantial grounds. Conferences and business functions catered for.

Separate 'Inn in the Park' at the rear serves bar meals. Separate family room. No dogs allowed.

Last orders for meals at 2pm (1.45 Sunday) and 9.30pm. Bar snacks only on Sunday evenings

Price: ££

▶ *filling station by the junction roundabout*

▶ *Between Junctions 60 and 61, the town of Bishop Middleham offers four pubs of some interest and charm, but they are awkward to reach.*

Durham A690 Consett (A691) **(62)**
official junction numbers cease at this point

A Ramside Hall
Hotel
Carrville
℗ (0191) 386 5282

A pebbledashed and crenellated confection consisting of country park, club and golf course. Bars, carvery, grill room and restaurant are open to the public.

Dogs and children allowed.

Last orders for restaurant meals at 1.30pm and 9.30pm (9pm on Sundays)

Price: £££; carvery ££

▶ *filling station nearby*

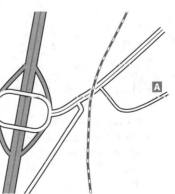

A690

to
Durham

Junctions **1** to **5**

It takes about ten minutes to cover this motorway; in fact it is the final part of the London–Portsmouth road which is dual carriageway almost the whole way from Putney Common, London, to the South Coast, linking into the A27/M27 between Havant and Portsmouth.

Pre-m'way junction Clanfield, Chalton
last junction before road achieves motorway status.

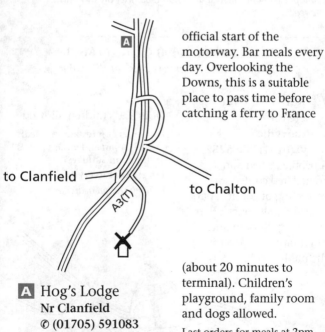

A official start of the motorway. Bar meals every day. Overlooking the Downs, this is a suitable place to pass time before catching a ferry to France

to Clanfield

A3(T)

to Chalton

A Hog's Lodge
Nr Clanfield
© (01705) 591083
A postwar brick and tiled country pub lying on the old largely disused A3 and about 2 miles from the

(about 20 minutes to terminal). Children's playground, family room and dogs allowed.

Last orders for meals at 2pm and 10pm (9.30 Sunday)
▶ *specialities: Sunday lunch choice of two roasts*
Price: £££

1 Horndean
start of motorway

A The Anchor
Horndean
© (01705) 591050

A 19th-century white village house, now a pub, offering morning coffee, bar snacks, lunches and dinners except Sunday and Monday evenings. Small enclosed front garden with outside seating. Children welcomed, but no play area, and dogs allowed.

Last orders for weekday meals at 2pm and 9pm. Sunday and Monday lunch only until 2pm

Price: ££; special prices available to pensioners

▶ *filling station nearby*

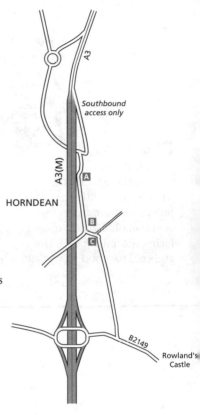

B Ship & Bell Hotel
Horndean
© (01705) 592107

Originally a 17th-century coaching inn belonging to the George Gale Brewery which it adjoins. Accommodation in 14 rooms; restaurant and two bars serving bar meals. A comfortable unostentatious country hotel where the condition of the beer may be relied upon. Children's playground; no dogs permitted.

Last orders for meals at 2.30pm and 9.30pm; Sunday lunch only

▶ *specialities: home cooking with much use of beer*

Price: £–££

C Red Lion
Horndean
✆ (01705) 593202

An attractive 18th-century pub and restaurant in the centre of old Horndean and facing the Ship & Bell. Hot and cold bar food served all day every day. Children's playground and family room. No dogs.

Open from 11.30am (midday Sunday) until 10pm

Price: ££

reader's response forms

The following reader response pages are for you to use to send us details about any pub or restaurant you think should be included in the next edition of **5 Minutes off the Motorway**.

We would also be delighted to receive any comments concerning existing entries.

Please remember to include your name and address on the reverse of the forms, which should be returned to:

▶ **5 Minutes off the Motorway: Reader Response**
Cadogan Books plc
London House
Parkgate Road
London SW11 4NQ

Senders of the best information will receive a Cadogan Guide of their choice.

reader's response

▶ I suggest the pub or restaurant below as a new entry for your next edition:

Pub/restaurant name:

Approximate location:

Motorway: Junction No.:

Any further details:

Pub/restaurant name:

Approximate location:

Motorway: Junction No.:

Any further details:

▶ I suggest the listing below be amended in the next edition:

Pub/restaurant name:

Motorway: Junction No.:

Suggested amendment:

▶ I suggest the listing below be deleted from the next edition:

Pub/restaurant name:

Motorway: Junction No.:

Reason for deletion:

---

reader's details

Name:

Address:

reader's response

▶ I suggest the pub or restaurant below as a new entry
for your next edition:

Pub/restaurant name:

Approximate location:

Motorway: Junction No.:

Any further details:

Pub/restaurant name:

Approximate location:

Motorway: Junction No.:

Any further details:

▶ I suggest the listing below be amended in the next edition:

Pub/restaurant name:

Motorway: **Junction No.:**

Suggested amendment:

▶ I suggest the listing below be deleted from the next edition:

Pub/restaurant name:

Motorway: **Junction No.:**

Reason for deletion:

---

reader's details

Name:

Address:

5 minutes off the motorway

reader's response

▶ I suggest the pub or restaurant below as a new entry for your next edition:

Pub/restaurant name:

Approximate location:

Motorway: Junction No.:

Any further details:

Pub/restaurant name:

Approximate location:

Motorway: Junction No.:

Any further details:

▶ I suggest the listing below be amended in the next edition:

Pub/restaurant name:

Motorway: Junction No.:

Suggested amendment:

▶ I suggest the listing below be deleted from the next edition:

Pub/restaurant name:

Motorway: Junction No.:

Reason for deletion:

---

reader's details

Name:

Address: